The Persuasive Manager
How to Sell Yourself and Your Ideas

The Persuasive Manager

How to Sell Yourself and Your Ideas

Thomas L. Quick

CHILTON BOOK COMPANY
Radnor, Pennsylvania

Library of Congress Cataloging in Publication Data
Quick, Thomas L.
  The persuasive manager.
  Includes index.
  1. Selling.   2. Persuasion (Psychology)
I. Title.
HF5438.25.Q5   658.8'5   80-70254
ISBN 0-8019-7074-1   AACR2

1 2 3 4 5 6 7 8 9 0   1 0 9 8 7 6 5 4 3 2

To Margaret V. Higginson

Contents

4 Developing a Persuasive State of Mind 37

5 Practicing the Fine Points of Persuasion 55

6 Selling Yourself and Your Ideas 70

7 Selling Against Opposition 89

8 Techniques that Resolve Conflict 107

9 Selling Bad News 124

10 Selling to a Group 144

11 Building Influence in Meetings　160

12 Selling and Successful Managing　180

Index　190

1

Getting Your Way

This book is about how to get more of what you want by influencing other people more effectively. It is designed to help you to accomplish more of your objectives, to improve the quality of your work and personal life, and to become more successful in your career.

You will want to read this book if you have ever:

- missed out on a promotion or desirable assignment that you believed yourself qualified for;
- wondered why no action was taken on a good idea you submitted to management;
- heard some of your proposals or opinions misquoted later by others;
- suspected that people were unwilling to listen to you;
- believed that others enjoy greater access to the powerful people in your organization;
- suspected that your co-workers take other people's ideas and opinions more seriously than yours;
- been frustrated by your lack of success in getting optimum performance from the people on your staff.

In short, if you have ever failed to achieve something you wanted very much, thought you were qualified for, or felt you were entitled to, this book can be useful to you.

Your failure to achieve these goals is probably *not* due to anything faulty in your ideas, suggestions, proposals, or thinking processes. There is probably nothing deficient about your talents and abilities, and you most likely have a pleasing personality, too. But you may be short on persuasive skills. In fact, most people's persuasive abilities are deficient, because the foundation of persuasiveness is basic selling skills. Most people haven't learned these skills and most people don't think of themselves as salespeople.

Nevertheless, everyone sells, including you. You sell yourself, your opinions and ideas, your work, your way of doing things. You are selling when you place yourself in the running for a job or promotion; sit on a committee and suggest a course of action or a solution to a problem; try to convince a neighbor to remove a dead tree from his side of the property line; ask for a raise or a transfer; run for office in the PTA or in a professional association; argue before higher management that your department should have responsibility for the new product; or ask your employees for increased effort. You are even selling when you argue your political views at a party.

What selling skills can do for you

You can use selling skills to build influence among your colleagues. Those same skills will help you achieve more visibility with people above you in the hierarchy. Selling techniques enable you to advance yourself and your ideas, to disarm your opposition, to resolve conflict or to reduce its likelihood. In a group decision-making situation, they can be invaluable in guiding the deliberation to the end you seek.

These skills have special significance for the manager of today's workforce, who increasingly respond positively to *sell* rather than *tell*. Employees want to be considered seriously, persuaded, negotiated with. The manager who knows how to deal with subordinates in these ways often achieves greater productivity, loyalty, and cooperation than managers who practice the more authoritarian style of management.

Unquestionably some people sell more effectively than others. You can see this in action every day at work. In your meetings, does everyone there get equal attention? Do their ideas get equal acceptance? No, of course not. Two participants may have good ideas, but chances are one is listened to more intently than the other. Two subordinates with similar abilities ask the boss for a raise; one gets it, one doesn't.

Some people can get on the telephone and round up volunteers or money much more successfully than others. Some managers enjoy an enviable amount of employee loyalty and commitment that other managers seem to lack. And the people on organizational fast tracks are invariably men and women who know how to sell themselves, to move faster than others to the more powerful positions, to make more money, to receive the juicy job offers.

Some super persuaders

Here are some particular examples of effective selling on the job. In one company, a certain project bounced around from one department to another. No one seemed to be able to get it off the ground. Finally, a young department head was asked to take it on, and he agreed—but only after negotiating a fat pay increase reflecting his new (and risky) responsibility. There was a lot of grumbling at his audacity—and much envy, too. He possessed not only a highly favorable image of himself but some effective selling skills as well.

In another organization, a middle manager persuaded management to write a job description solely for himself and to create a separate salary grade in which he was the only qualifier. Another superb salesman I recall was anxious to get out of his company's training program and take over a branch office. But management was anxious to take advantage of his exceptional analytical and mathematical skills in the home office for a time. They wound up paying a price: he insisted upon receiving the title of assistant sales manager, this before doing a day of selling in the field.

Other examples of super sales jobs are even more remarkable. For instance, the recently retired chairman of one of the largest life insurance companies in the United States started out as a group insurance specialist in a relatively small department. While he was group sales manager, his department suffered several years of losses. Nonetheless, due in large part to superb sales skills, he moved up to become the first non-actuary chief executive of the company. Granted, he had been trained as a salesman. But what is significant is that he applied, within the organization, what he had learned in the field.

A few years back, one psychologist-author literally drove his book onto the bestseller list by traveling all over the country with copies of the book, badgering managers of radio and television stations to grant him interview time, and convincing bookstore owners to take his book on consignment.

A young black engineer became mayor of an eastern city when it was virtually bankrupt and devastated by riots. He succeeded in persuading the factions—black and white—to work together to save the city. That was one monumental selling job. Another example is the president of an ailing airline who persuaded employees to accept pay cuts to help turn the company around, despite the strength of the unions and the reputedly low morale throughout the workforce.

As these examples show, there are few situations in which you cannot profitably use selling skills, the same skills that salespeople use to persuade prospects to buy their products or services. Selling, after all, is the way things are accomplished. In fact, Red Motley, one-time publisher of *Parade* magazine, said, "Nothing happens until someone sells something."

If selling is so important, if it can help people to achieve so many desirable ends, then why are so many people relatively ineffective in their persuasiveness?

Three barriers to persuasion

There are many reasons why people have problems getting others to go along with their ideas or accept their proposals. Most of these reasons can be grouped under three categories:

1. What they say

A common mistake many people make is to "let the facts speak for themselves." Facts seldom speak for themselves. Someone has to tell their story for them. Unfortunately, some people have the firm conviction that if you line up enough points of fact, people will be persuaded. An excessive reliance on content often produces the MEGO effect (my eyes glaze over). Furthermore, the facts that people select to present are those that usually reflect their own values and priorities. They would be effective in persuading the would-be persuader, but not necessarily anyone else.

2. How they say it

Many people build communication barriers by using words, gestures, or speech patterns that distract or mystify others. Their disorganized remarks leave others confused about what points they are trying to make. Sometimes they simply bore their audience. Seldom do most people ask themselves before a presentation, interview, or transaction, "How can I organize these facts or thoughts to achieve the impact that I want?"

3. How they follow up

Many people, after they have pressed others to accept what they have proposed, drop the initiative or give up control. Or they may achieve agreement but then fail to nail down a course of action. Thus many agreements are made, but never acted upon. Others don't know how to handle opposition—they collapse, or become defensive or argumentative. Or they compromise when they don't want to or don't have to.

Another important reason why many people fail to persuade is that they have an aversion to "selling." We will deal with this in the next section.

Overcoming the stigma of selling

Unfortunately, when you mention selling, many people show distaste. There is a stigma attached to selling, an unflattering stereotype of the salesperson. Selling is something equated with manipulating, deceiving, being devious, being a huckster. For the most part, though, that equation is wrong.

Few salespeople today would countenance cheating, deception, or dishonesty of any sort. The good sale is a transaction—open, above-board, into which the parties enter willingly and knowingly in order to gain something of value to both. Successful selling does not take place at the expense of the buyer. Looking out for Number One, or being selfish, is seldom advantageous to the seller because it means that the seller must "leave town" after the sale. Trickery destroys trust and credibility.

Chances are, most of the salespeople with whom you have done business were knowledgeable about what they were selling, probably low-key, and avoided anything resembling pressure. Furthermore, if you reflect, people who've sold you probably were not bombastic, jolly, extroverted. Some of the best salespeople I have known and worked with are quietly intelligent, sometimes even introverted, thoughtful, and attentive. They just didn't fit the stereotype.

My purpose in rebutting the stereotype is so that I may use the words *selling* and *selling skills* freely without conjuring up negative reactions. Because selling, successful persuasion, is what this book is all about.

These, then, are the premises of this book:

1. You have a right to go after what you want or need for yourself or your company.

2. People who have persuasive powers generally have a better chance of getting what they want than those who do not.

3. You can develop persuasive powers by sharpening your selling skills. And this book will help you do it.

What makes some people so influential?

If by now you agree that virtually everyone is selling something some of the time, then you must also ask the question, "Why are some people so much better at it than others?"

I'll answer that question in this book—and show you how you can be one of those who are better at it. But it might be useful to list some characteristics of people who have better-than-average persuasive powers. For example:

1. They know what they want

This is no small thing. They have goals. And they are careful not to lose sight of those goals. In modern psychological parlance, they *own* their wants. They want to win, although they are realistic enough to know that they cannot consistently win at the expense of others.

2. They know they have a right to try to get what they want

The successful salesperson tends to believe that he or she has a right to make a sales presentation, and that belief is often what gets the salesperson through the door. It would never occur to an experienced representative to think, "I don't have a right to ask for an appointment, for a chance to tell my story." Of course, no salesperson is going to conclude that he or she also has a right to get an order. That depends on the person's selling skills, not the least of which is the ability to recognize the needs and wants of the prospect and to meet them with the product or scrvice.

Much the same thing can be said of you. You may not necessarily have the right to get your plan approved, your solution accepted, your ideas adopted, or your promotion granted, but you certainly have the right to speak your mind, to offer yourself or your ideas.

3. They are articulate

Not only do persuasive people know what they want, they know how to express those wants. They may not use the words "I want," but they know how to translate their wants and needs into terms that others can accept. As you will see in subsequent chapters, effective persuaders realize that poorly chosen words and gestures can build barriers to understanding or acceptance by others. They are careful to avoid creating such barriers.

4. They are sensitive

Successful persuaders are sensitive to what others might want from and contribute to the transaction. They are skillful at sensing the verbal and nonverbal language of others. More important, they strive to involve others. Assertion, after all, is only one aspect of effective persuading. The expert persuader knows that the other person, the "buyer," must be involved, and that the other person must be a participant in the transaction. Successful salespeople question their prospects and encourage them to talk to increase their involvement in the transaction. The other person has something to contribute— knowledge, experience, ideas, needs, and resources, all of which can be helpful to you. If you do not involve the other, there will be little or no communication and understanding; certainly there will be no persuasion.

Experienced persuaders are also sensitive to time and situation. There is a time and place for everything, and they are ever alert to how, when, and where to go after certain kinds of actions, decisions, or requests.

5. They have credibility

Influential people develop a reputation for dealing squarely. Without abandoning their own interests, they are careful not to ride roughshod over those of others. Persuading is usually not a matter of winning friends. To influence others, you do not have to be loved. But you must be respected and trusted. Credibility is probably the single most important characteristic of the successful persuader. Real believability takes time to build, but not very long to destroy.

Credibility has to do with others' trust in you. Your listeners must be confident that you will not knowingly deceive them. Making a mistake in fact or judgment is one thing—one the people you work with will probably forgive you for—but if you are guilty of deception or falsifying, you may find your credibility shattered beyond repair.

Credibility, as I've indicated, is much more important than likeability. In fact, some very persuasive people, successful salespeople even, are not warm and genial. They may be even gruff and distant. But in working with them, you are aware that they will not ignore your interests in the transaction. They may not be trying to win friends, but they are looking after their interests, and that usually involves yours as well. At the very least, you know that in looking after their interests, they will not knowingly violate yours by deception.

6. They know how to deal with opposition

People who are skilled at persuading others anticipate opposition and know how to handle it. They even welcome a certain amount of open opposition—because hidden opposition is virtually impossible to deal with. Also, objections openly expressed can be tested and verified. If the objections are real, then the persuader has learned something, and knows exactly what he or she has to do to win the objective. Obviously handling opposition effectively depends upon getting the other person involved in the transaction.

Successful persuaders come prepared for a "hard sell," if necessary, but they never let their "worst case" scenarios stand in the way of responsive communication with the other. Their responses to objections are geared to keeping the door to communication and persuasion open.

7. They know how to ask for the order

A satisfying transaction has a beginning, a middle, and an end. The end is the closure—the bid for action. Those transactions that don't close are very frustrating to the people involved. One situation comes readily to mind. Years ago, two men had a falling out, and today, although neither can remember the cause of the dispute, they remain antagonistic. Neither seems to know how to resolve the conflict, to achieve closure.

Other examples are the project planning that continues interminably without leading anywhere, or the idea that is submitted to management and disappears into the organizational machinery. It's never pronounced dead, but it's never actualized either.

Another case is the group that becomes so comfortable with a problem that it resists attempts to solve it. Discussing it time after time makes participants feel as if they are accomplishing something and provides a good reason (*i.e.*, no time) not to tackle other issues.

We have all experienced "no action" situations like those described above. Nevertheless, people have an urge to complete a task or a transaction. They want to close it out so that, with a fresh and open mind, they can move on to something else. Good selling techniques provide ways to close. Every salesperson is trained to "ask for the order." A sales presentation cannot be considered complete without something resulting from the effort, if only an agreement to set another appointment. (The actual contract may not come for a long time.) But the issue of closure is this: What should be considered the culmination of this step, so that I (we) can go on to the next step?

8. They know what motivates others

Good persuaders understand that what motivates people to act is 1) perceived value of the result of the action, and 2) accessibility or ease of achievement of the goal. Confronted by a choice of two options, people tend to select the one that is more valuable to them. But value is not the only consideration. Equally important is the question, "Can I really get it?" If it is a question of expense, for example, a salesperson will suggest terms of payment. If the prospect questions his ability to use a product, the salesperson offers instruction. If the prospect doubts the benefits of the plan, the salesperson offers reassurance.

These two factors, value and probability of success in attaining the reward, are central to motivation theory. For the prospect to "buy" a product or an idea, he or she must value the result and believe that it is attainable. The successful persuader uncovers the value and makes it possible for the other person to have and enjoy it.

In summary, then, when persuasive people have an idea, proposal, or opinion, they:

- make it interesting—otherwise, whatever is being said won't be listened to;
- make it valuable—it must appeal to the self-interests of others;
- make it easy—if it isn't seen as do-able, then it won't be done.

2

How the Sales Pro Does It

There is a myth that salespeople are born, not made. The implication is that the very persuasive person enjoys some sort of genetically coded gift. While it is true that some people take to selling more easily than others, most successful salespeople get that way through hard work. They are continually expanding their knowledge of what they sell, of human behavior, and of people's needs, and they are constantly sharpening their awareness of what is going on at any given moment among the people engaged in the transaction.

In the pages that follow, you have the opportunity to follow a professional at work. As you see what she does in a sales situation, note how many of her skills can be applied to non-sales transactions. You may be surprised to see how much skill and training the selling process actually takes.

Sheila Layton sells a planning service to high-level executives in small and medium-size corporations. Sheila's company prepares up-to-date reports showing economic trends, legal developments that may constrain corporate activities, research data that indicate new markets and buyer trends, and other information that helps corporate executives plan their marketing strategy for the next year or two. It is a very sophisticated and somewhat costly service. It is a "hard sell," because Sheila must not only sell the product, she must help create in her prospects' minds the sense that they need the product and can benefit from the investment of nearly $800 per year.

Sheila uses a fairly standard sales presentation that she has developed through the years. If she is not interrupted, she can cover it completely in twenty-two minutes. Sheila knows that within the first ten minutes, she must offer enough benefits to arouse the prospect's interest. Thus, when she asks an executive over the telephone for an appointment, she is prepared to say, if he resists, that within ten minutes he will know whether it is worth his while to let her have the other twelve minutes.

The approach

Sheila's usual approach on the phone goes like this:

SHEILA: Mr. Leventhal? This is Sheila Layton of Federated Strategic Services. I'd like to arrange to meet with you for a few minutes to show you how our Executive's Planning System can help you increase your profits. I wonder whether 9:30 Tuesday morning would be convenient for you, or would 3:30 Wednesday be better?

LEVENTHAL: This is our busy time. And it really doesn't sound as if I'd be interested.

SHEILA: I can understand why you'd feel that way. If you weren't busy, I don't think it would be in your interest to see me. A number of companies in this area are already using our system, and what we hear from them is that it saves time and makes money for them. It will only take me a few minutes to show you how it can benefit you. Would Tuesday morning be convenient or shall we make it Wednesday afternoon?

LEVENTHAL: I don't know. Anyway, I'll be with a customer on Tuesday.

SHEILA: Would Wednesday at 3:30 be better? Or how about Friday at 9:00? I'll guarantee, Mr. Leventhal, that within ten minutes you'll know enough to say to me, "That's enough," or "Give me the rest." Ten minutes, that's all.

LEVENTHAL: Make it Friday.

Sheila does not give any more information on the telephone than she has to, knowing that people often look for a way to say no. She therefore abstains from giving any information which could lead an executive to decide not to see her. She is aware that what she is selling at this time is the appointment only. No matter how much pressure is exerted on her by the prospect, she avoids selling the service by phone or giving him an easy way to say no. Note that she conscientiously observes the three precepts of selling. Sheila makes the appointment interesting and valuable for Mr. Levanthal: other companies are using the service (possibly gaining an advantage over him) and making money. Sheila makes it easy: a maximum of only ten minutes for him to know whether he wants to know more. In addition, she offers specific times for him to choose from, drawing him away from the alternative, namely not to see her at all.

Observation: Persuasion is often done in stages, and at each stage there is a "product." The product of the first stage is getting the agreement of the other person to set aside time to listen. When you approach a colleague or a higher-level executive with an idea, you may be seriously disadvantaged if you offer too much information on that first approach. Sell the idea of listening to you by giving just enough information to arouse interest: "I've been playing around with some ideas that might help us reduce our cost of materials, and I'd like to get together with you. Would you have a few minutes this afternoon?" Resist the invitation to give your "presentation" in a corridor or to "Write me a memo." If you must write a memo, keep in mind that you want an appointment, not a decision. Tailor your information accordingly.

The discovery period

By the time Sheila shows up in the lobby of Mr. Leventhal's company, she will have done some homework—how large the company is, its products or services, its markets. But the learning must continue. What further information can she discover?

A salesperson often gets a feel for the company even in the lobby. For example, is the lobby comfortable? Companies that welcome visitors or are concerned about their image to outsiders will usually go to the trouble of creating a comfortable and inviting environment in their lobbies. Often, too, the company attitude toward visitors will be reflected in how the receptionist interacts with them. Has she been trained to make them feel welcome and to help them? Or does she feel free to treat them as if they are intruders? These clues may prepare the salesperson for the kind of reception waiting inside.

How is Sheila introduced to Mr. Leventhal? Does he come out? Send someone? Does he stay behind his desk as if seeking protection? Does he open himself up to a new acquaintance—or build barriers? What is his office like?

Sheila is taking everything in that might be a clue to what kind of person Mr. Leventhal might be. This is a time of discovery. Mr. Leventhal may buy, but if he does, it will not be on strictly rational terms. Everything that she can learn about Mr. Leventhal the person as well as Mr. Leventhal the executive will help.

On the ideal sales call, Mr. Leventhal would get up and greet Sheila with a warm smile and firm handshake. Conversation would flow easily, she would sense that her presentation would go smoothly, and a sale would be completed quickly. But this is the ideal, not the norm.

The salesperson usually has to warm the prospect up first, to get him or her more relaxed and receptive to the sales presentation. And each prospect is different. Each one is a unique personality and puts an individual stamp on the way business is conducted. Furthermore, each prospect is subjected to varying external pressures. For example, just before the sales interview one prospect might have discovered the loss of a major customer. A cold may be making another prospect miserable. Still another might have quarreled with her spouse at breakfast.

Such extraneous factors can influence buying motivations. No one can always be privy to their precise nature, but to be successful, the salesperson must adjust the presentation to the prospect's needs *and* mood. For greater effectiveness, this adjustment should be made *before* the presentation is begun, or, at least, in its early stages.

Respecting personal space

In any transaction, it is important to recognize and respect personal space. Each person creates a private zone, an area they call their own, in which they feel secure. Some people, for example, zealously protect their privacy by ceasing to respond when your questions or comments become too personal. Others may rely more on physical distance. If you stand too close to them, they back off.

Sheila knows it is important not to invade a prospect's space, because that person will be uncomfortable, distracted, perhaps even resentful. Those are hardly the elements that form a good selling atmosphere.

Does Mr. Leventhal feel more comfortable with Sheila sitting across the desk or beside it? (She might prefer to sit at the side of the desk, but if there is no chair placed there, she has a pretty good clue about his preferences.) Is he informal in his greeting, or reserved? Does he shake hands warmly? All of these indicate how much space he wants to preserve. Taking these cues, Sheila will vary her selling approach—more formal, less formal, more questions, fewer questions, even how she will modulate her voice. If Mr. Leventhal seems to wish to maintain some distance, she will modulate her voice, adjust her questions, and be careful to keep her hands away from the work area of his desk when she uses visual material.

The space question is just as vital in an interaction with someone you know well as with someone you don't. In fact, it may be a greater factor where the acquaintanceship is established. With a stranger, you are understandably wary. With someone you know, you may unthinkingly invade space, taking liberties such as standing too close or touching when those actions are unwelcome.

A word about dealing with subordinates. Managers sometimes forget how important it is to respect the space of people who work for them. They interrupt subordinates' conversation, enter offices without knocking, consider others' work areas to be extensions of their own. These thoughtless actions can create barriers that inhibit communicating.

Conversation starters

In order to sell successfully, Sheila needs information on her prospect. Obviously, the best source is the prospect himself. Unfortunately, if this is the first meeting, that source may not be inclined to volunteer this information. Consequently, through the use of subtle warm-up techniques, the salesperson must get the conversation started.

In choosing a conversation-opening device that can effectively warm up the prospect, Sheila considers several things. First of all, will her opener get the prospect to talk; is it related to the prospect's interests? Some examples: pictures on the wall that show the prospect in a significant event or with a well-known person, certificates of achievement, awards, or books may point to a particular interest of the prospect. Other devices have to do with the business—a reported high accomplishment, a recent acquisition, an industry trend.

Secondly, will the device create the climate for specific questions? Sheila is not looking for a pleasant chat that could sidetrack her selling efforts. She wants to get Mr. Leventhal talking, true, but she wants the opening conversation to permit her to ask specific questions that elicit the kinds of data that could be helpful to her.

Third, will the opener provide a logical bridge to the sales presentation? Nothing is more disconcerting than for the salesperson or the prospect to indicate, "Well, this is very pleasant talk, but time is passing; let's get to work." Instead, Sheila always looks for a tie-in. "What you said a minute ago, Mr. Leventhal, about tighter budgets this year is a concern that many executives such as you are expressing, and that's why a number of them—people you know, I'm sure—are finding that our system takes some of the pressure off. Let me show you how it works."

There are always some prospects who resist supplying information the salesperson needs. Yet getting the right information or response from a prospect is one key to sales success. To counter such resistance, here are some approaches that Sheila might use.

The key-question technique

Asking a couple of hard, intelligent questions is an ideal approach for the no-nonsense type of prospect, the kind who says, "My time is limited." When this happens, the response can be: "I can appreciate that, Mr. Leventhal. And I have a few key questions that will help us get down to business very quickly."

This approach puts Sheila on the spot, not the prospect, and she must deliver by asking questions that count. Prospects in this category are likely to respect tough questions, so Sheila should be prepared to ask them: "Mr. Leventhal, will anyone else in the company have to approve this purchase, should you be in favor of it?

The give-credit technique

Sometimes a prospect will say something that raises an important question in the salesperson's mind. It is better for Sheila to move in while the point is hot, give the prospect credit, and ask: "Mr. Leventhal, that is a crucial point you just made. Can you tell me . . . ?"

The silent technique

There are times when prospects talk but don't really say enough. Their answers to questions may be brief or unsatisfactory. In such instances, when prospects stop talking, Sheila simply says, "Mmmm. . . ." Then she looks thoughtful, remains silent, and waits. Usually, prospects will break the silence and elaborate on what they have been saying.

Observation: If you call upon someone whom you do not know very well, whether in your organization or outside, applying some of Sheila's discovery techniques can work for you in getting clues as to what kind of person you are talking with. In almost every case, it is possible to take a minute or two to warm the person up. Chat about something that has happened in the company, or relay some news of someone you both know. The point is that the other person has been occupied with other matters, and your warm-up can provide a "disconnect" that allows him or her to switch away from other items to you.

The three bridging techniques described above can be useful to you in further arousing the interest of your "prospect." Here is the kind of "key question" you might ask: "I'm getting the impression that there is growing interest around here in experimenting with quality circles. Am I right?" What you are persuading the other to do at this point is to take sufficient time to listen to you and to get involved with your ideas.

Furthermore, taking a minute or two before launching into your story can help you to assess the mood of the other person. You may want to revise the remarks you had intended to make, eliminate some, add others, to suit the other person's state of mind.

As you may suspect, much of the groundwork for a sale is done before the actual presentation begins. The warm-up period relaxes the prospect, enables him or her to begin to trust this stranger, to believe what the salesperson says. If the salesperson does a poor job in conveying the message, "I am here to provide good things for you (as well as for myself)," then the sale may never be made.

During the presentation

It is during the presentation itself that observing the three precepts—interesting, valuable, easy—is vital. Sheila makes it valuable from the beginning by at least describing some of the benefits that Leventhal will enjoy from the service that Sheila's company provides. "Fast action on just one of our recommendations could mean savings to you of thousands of dollars." "So complete is our coverage (*a feature*) that you can sleep soundly at night knowing that you're on top of external developments that can provide you with opportunities to increase your profits or that could cut into them (*a feature translated into a benefit*)." After promising benefits Sheila explains how the system works.

Her presentation is interesting in that she tells what Leventhal needs to know without much repetition or elaboration. If she swamps him with too much information or too many details, her presentation not only becomes boring, but it permits no questions. Leventhal's questions indicate what elements of the system interest him most. Not only do his questions get him involved, but they could be potential buying signals.

Sheila has eliminated dead spots in her presentation, spots that she has found boring to say. She uses as many one-syllable words as possible, avoiding jargon and technical language. She varies the speed of her delivery, pausing now and then. But in general, she moves the presentation along rather quickly. (Interestingly, some studies have shown that people who speak more rapidly than average have more credibility with their listeners.)

During the actual presentation, Sheila will watch Leventhal's reactions to what she is saying. That is one advantage of knowing the presentation well: it leaves the salesperson free to concentrate on picking up clues and reactions in the prospect. She uses a visual aid, in a large three-ring binder, the pages of which she turns slowly and carefully. She is careful not to talk to the notebook but to Leventhal. Eye contact is very important—not a stare, but frequent contact.

Sheila works to involve her prospect in what is going on. If she sees him nodding or looking very thoughtful, she will expand the point she is explaining and then seek a reaction. "Does this make sense to you, Mr. Leventhal?" Or, "I would imagine that, considering your type of business, you would find this aspect of our system especially useful, am I correct?" Or, "Do you have any questions up to this point, Mr. Leventhal?"

If she is unable to get much response, she might choose to slow down the presentation and to summarize periodically, because she has no clear indication that her prospect is really following her closely.

Observation: A frequent mistake people make, especially when they work together, is to present ideas in a spontaneous manner. When you have an important idea or proposal, develop a presentation. It shows the other that you have done your homework. It enhances interest, because you cut down on repetition and rambling, thereby saving time. Many good ideas get buried because they are presented in a disorganized, uninteresting manner. Furthermore, when you are sure what you are going to say, you can stay more alert to the reactions of your listener.

The closure

The closure is your bid for action. One reason so many excellent ideas never get beyond the talking stage is that people presenting them don't ask for action. They arouse interest, sell the data—and then let it die. How is your idea to be realized? Who will be responsible? In what time frame? You have not persuaded anyone until you have secured a commitment to action.

If Leventhal gets involved or shows more than average interest, Sheila may attempt to get an early commitment from him (a trial close), even though her presentation is not finished. There are a number of ways to close. To illustrate, let's assume Leventhal makes it clear that one of the periodic analyses that comes from Federal is especially relevant to him. Sheila explores this with him to reinforce its usefulness to him. She may ask him which of the other parts of the system that she has covered would also be useful. By this means she is encouraging him to think about the system in a positive way. He focuses on *how* he can use it rather than on *whether*. Then Sheila closes.

SHEILA: I can see, Mr. Leventhal, that this one regular analysis alone would guarantee your making a profitable investment. All the other reports and analyses would constitute a bonus for you. (*If he agrees, she places an order form before him.*) We're talking about an investment of $ _____ per month. For that you'll reeceive (*she summarizes briefly*). As you can see, that's roughly $4 per report. And I'm sure you'll agree, one bit of help can quickly return your investment. I can get this started for you by the first of the month if you'll just give me your okay here.

With the pen Sheila points out where he is to sign, and then she places it near him. That's making it easy. Note that she doesn't ask him to sign, just to give her an okay, which seems to be less binding and legal.

Probably one of the following three things will happen: 1) Leventhal will pick up the pen and sign the order; 2) he will say, "Let me hear the rest"; 3) or he will ask a question or voice an objection or uncertainty that is in the way of his doing business with her.

If number 2 is the reaction, Sheila will continue her presentation. Number 3 is valuable because Sheila has smoked out an obstacle to buying. She might choose to try to answer the objection or clear up the uncertainty somewhere in the final part of the presentation, or she might wait to see whether it comes up again. When Sheila finishes the presentation, she will probably summarize the principal benefits of the system and ask once again for the order.

She has observed the three precepts of motivating the buyer: she made it interesting, she stressed the value, and she made it easy to approve the order.

But suppose Leventhal doesn't buy. Instead, the following takes place:

LEVENTHAL: I don't know. It's a good system, and it's certainly very complete. I'm not sure, though, that I would get my money's worth.

SHEILA: Well, if you're not sure that you would get your money's worth, of course you'd hesitate. Here is something, Mr. Leventhal, that many of our subscribers find especially valuable to them. I touched on it before, but I'm sure you'd like to know why it has special value. (*Sheila selects a benefit to describe again, perhaps more fully, probably with a verbal proof story—an actual case in which a subscriber used the service in a specific way and reaped a good return on the subscription price.*) This is the kind of return that I'm sure you can realize from our system if you let me get it started for you. By the way, this report that I was talking about is available. I'm sure I can get it for you at no additional cost. Shall I order it?

LEVENTHAL: It's very tempting. I know I would find it interesting. But just how useful, I don't know.

SHEILA: I see.

The value objection has come up twice. Sheila can respond to it now, or she can try another close. If she chooses the latter, she will select another benefit to summarize, perhaps another proof story. Then she will describe a special easy payment plan and once again ask Leventhal to buy.

If Leventhal again resists, Sheila will probably try to dig out a more specific objection. Here is an approach she might use: "In our discussion you've indicated that you have found some aspects of our system both interesting and potentially useful to you. What are some of the ways that you believe our system might have value to you?"

She is encouraging Leventhal to think in a positive way. He will probably respond, describing what parts of the program he likes. But even though he sees things that he likes, he still hesitates.

SHEILA: I'm convinced by what you say that you see quite a bit of value here. But there is a reservation in your mind. What stands between us and doing business, Mr. Leventhal?

LEVENTHAL: It is interesting, and there might be something here for me. But sometimes I have to wear many hats. I get very busy. Something like this would pile up on my desk, and it would be wasted.

SHEILA: So you're concerned about missing an item that could be profitable to you?

LEVENTHAL: Of course.

SHEILA: And if you knew that there was something in that pile that could be profitable, and if you knew just where it was, you'd certainly take a look at it, wouldn't you?

LEVENTHAL: Yes, sure.

SHEILA: Fine. I know a lot of busy executives like you must conserve your time as carefully as possible. This is why we developed this format. Under each section is a brief one- or two-sentence summary of what follows in the copy. (*Sheila demonstrates a typical report or analysis. She is emphasizing a feature, namely the format of the report. In selling, features such as color, shape, format are incidental, but a skillful salesperson can turn a feature into a benefit. And Sheila does.*) All you have to do is to open the envelope, glance at the summaries, and you'll know within 30 seconds whether there is something that applies to you right now. That's all—thirty seconds. If you can spare half a minute, why don't you give me your okay to go ahead. (*She makes sure pen and order form are convenient to her prospect.*)

Silence. Sheila says no more. In fact, every time she has closed, she has fallen silent. Silence is a potent factor in the close. Once the salesperson has talked, asked for action, and stopped talking, the burden is squarely on the prospect. The continuing silence of the salesperson keeps it there. Eventually the prospect has to do something. Silence creates some stress. To relieve the stress, the prospect moves. Sometimes it's a yes, sometimes a no.

Sheila could also have used silence effectively when Leventhal was giving his reasons for not buying. When a salesperson looks interested, maintains eye contact, does not speak, the prospect is often impelled to keep talking. The salesperson's body language, the listening, the silence, all say to the prospect that more explanation is anticipated. Very often, the real objection comes tumbling out.

Fielding objections

You will recall that Sheila did not attempt to answer Leventhal's objection on the first go-around. For one thing, she does not know how serious the objection is. If it really is not a strong one, she does not want to reinforce it by dealing with it seriously. Also, she knows full well that genuine objections often do not surface early on. It may be that the prospect does not really have a strong objection; rather he or she simply hasn't been sold, hasn't been pushed to the point of saying yes. In this case any old excuse will do. The prospect isn't likely to say, "You haven't sold me," because that is going to invite more selling. Instead he says, "I really don't have the money" or "My situation is unique; it wouldn't help me" or "We're satisfied with our present supplier."

Other times the person hearing the presentation does not have the authority to buy. But instead of volunteering that information, some other excuse is made.

There are all sorts of reasons a person will give for not buying. If the prospect isn't sold and wants to stall, he or she will say something like, "I need to think about it" or "Come back in six months when things are better" or "I need to talk to my partner (spouse, boss, etc.)." A salesperson usually handles a stall in the same manner as an objection: resell the benefits and close.

The selling process

Sheila is a successful persuader. Many of her techniques can serve you well. For example:

Sell in stages

Hook your prospect so that you can arrange a presentation time. Sell the time and attention first, rather than the idea.

Set the tone

This you do by assessing the needs and wants of the other person as far as you can discover them. Pick up your clues wherever you can. Keep your discussion formal or informal as the situation and the prospect warrant.

Involve your prospect

Ask questions, get opinions, encourage reactions. You do this during the warm-up or the discovery period as well as during the presentation.

Give a well-organized presentation

Win your listener's attention with a well-thought-out presentation. Organize your ideas. Know what you want to say and how you want to say it, and give enough information for your listener to come to a decision.

Ask for action

Know what you would like to see happen as a result of the presentation and press for it. You have not persuaded anyone until you get some kind of commitment to action.

Don't be put off by opposition

You will usually experience some opposition any time you try to present a new idea or make a change. Sheila's responses to objections and stalls are applicable to most situations you will face. It is important to your persuasive skills that you know how to handle opposition. This subject will be dealt with more extensively in Chapter 7.

3

The Foundations of Persuasiveness

In the last chapter, you read how an experienced sales representative influences her prospect. The difference between Sheila Layton and most people who are not "professional persuaders" is that she is trained to think through each step of the process, and they are not. In each situation she works hard to practice five basic rules of persuasion. Everyone must follow these rules if they are to be successful in influencing other people.

Five rules of persuasion

1. Know your product

What idea, project, solution, or opinion are you selling? Perhaps you are hoping to persuade others to accept you for a job, promotion, or honor. Whatever you are selling, be confident that you know what you have to offer. What are the strengths, the benefits? Why should others buy you or your ideas? You cannot reasonably hope to persuade anyone or anything until you have first been able to convince them that you know what you are talking about.

An important part of knowing your product is being able to anticipate how those whom you are hoping to influence view it. Let's say you make a bid for a more responsible position in your organization. You are the product. You have a very good idea about what is required at that level, and you are convinced that you have the capabilities to handle those requirements. But your product knowledge is not complete until you try to develop a profile of you as the decision-makers see you. Specifically, how do they judge your demonstrated strengths and performance where you are now?

Similarly, if you are proposing to develop a new project, you must consider that you as well as the project are the product. Therefore, you have to look at your performance on previous projects as your "buyers" might see it.

2. *Know your prospect*

You have to know, or learn, something of the other person's needs and wants. That information is essential if you are to translate what you want into benefits that are attractive to your prospect. What parts of your proposition would interest him or her? Just as important, how would you describe those benefits? What kinds of words would you use? Is this a good time for your prospect to hear what you have to say? Would he or she be more receptive on another occasion, in another place? What tone of voice would you use? How detailed should you be—can you briefly sketch it or must you be thorough? Should your approach be formal or informal, friendly or professional? The answers to these questions are to be found in your knowledge of the other person.

Remember that persuasion does not occur entirely on a rational level. Your listener will respond to your presentation in a number of ways—rationally, emotionally, and intuitively—and it is essential to be able to anticipate some of these responses. People have biases, psychological sets, and preconceptions that you must be sensitive to. If you, say, have a Ph.D. and are trying to sell a program to the president of your corporation who is sensitive about his limited education, you will have to take pains to de-emphasize the breadth of your academic knowledge in making your presentation.

Every salesperson knows that sales, even to engineers, are seldom made solely on the specifications. I can remember from my own career in selling group insurance that much substantial business was obtained through bidding. But no set of specifications was ever airtight. There was always room for interpretation and flexibility. Clauses in contracts differed slightly, and the personal element was never completely absent. Some salespeople were more trustworthy than others, more pleasant to do business with than others, and the prospect could usually find ways to justify giving the contract to this person instead of that one.

3. Involve your prospect

Communication, in most cases, cannot flow one way. As I have indicated, the other person brings ideas, biases, strengths, wants, and needs to the transaction, and you need to hear them if they affect your getting what you want. Besides, you need to get feedback on how well you are doing in your persuasion. So take the prospect's temperature from time to time. Ask questions: "Does this make sense to you?" "Am I correct in assuming that . . . ?" Invite responses. Create a dialogue rather than a monologue.

Another reason you need to get the other person involved in your presentation is that many people have trouble listening. They are not trained to listen well. They tend to hear only part of what you say, or what they wish to hear—which may be quite different from what you are saying. Through your questions and invitation to respond, you can find out what they have heard.

Even people who listen well may have limited attention spans. If you don't change pace, if you don't get their participation, their minds wander.

4. Ask for action

The politician doesn't just shake hands. He asks people to vote for him. Don't forget or be hesitant to let the other person know what you want to happen as a result of the dialogue. Do you want help, a recommendation, a favor, advice, acceptance of your ideas, acceptance of you personally? Make sure you spell it out. Don't assume that your prospect always knows what you are selling or what you expect of him.

Many people dread the moment when they ask, in effect "Yes or no?" They are afraid that they will be rejected. So they often settle for no action, no conclusion. Inexperienced salespeople often buy stalls and accept indefinite answers in lieu of outright turndowns. But an experienced rep will push for a definite answer—even if it's a "no."

Remember also that asking for action provides closure for both of you and may relieve tension or uncertainty. Closure is both natural and desired. Have you ever had a colleague say to you about a visitor, "He took an hour of my time, and I still have no idea of what he wants?" Few things are more frustrating than a transaction that has no end.

5. Be prepared to handle opposition

When two or more people meet to discuss an issue for the first time, there is bound to be disagreement, at least initially. Besides, opposition to new and outside ideas is natural to many people. Few people listen attentively, surmount their biases easily, and surrender to someone else's ideas. A certain opposition, or at least hesitancy, is to be expected.

Unfortunately many people tend to take opposition personally. They believe that it is directed against them as persons, not against the ideas. Even if part of the opposition *is* personal, opposition usually indicates the need to do more skillful persuading. A positive way to look at opposition—the way many salespeople look at it—is to recognize that the person who is fighting you is involved. Nothing is worse than the prospect who ignores you.

Being persuasive is knowing the techniques and what makes them work and then applying them effectively. The techniques themselves are rather simple. But thinking them and applying them are more complicated. "Thinking them" means being aware of them, having the intention to use them, and to use them skillfully. It is almost as if you must think of yourself as a salesperson working to make sales. Unfortunately, most people don't think of themselves in that light. And because they don't, they get in their own way. In the rest of this chapter we'll look at examples of self-imposed obstacles to successful persuasion, and then we'll see how a transaction could be handled more effectively using the five rules described above.

Self-imposed obstacles

In the following exchange between a manager and his boss, the would-be persuader has a poor opener, has misjudged his prospect, and fails to adjust his approach in spite of cues from the boss— altogether a fatal combination.

MANAGER: You know, I was thinking that Edith has been complaining for some time that she hasn't gotten along with some of the people in Scheduling.

BOSS: Right. I'm aware of that.

MANAGER: Well, my first inclination was to tell Edith that she'd have to find a way to solve the problem. After all, other people have to learn to get along. But then, I realized how long it might take, and why continue to go through this when there might be another way? Don't you agree?

BOSS: Is there another way?

MANAGER: It's a funny coincidence. I happened to be talking to Stanley the other day, and, you know, he isn't really happy where he is, either.

BOSS: So?

MANAGER: Well, Stanley has had a lot of experience in Scheduling. Before we put Edith on the job . . . .

Finally, the boss is about to find out what the bottom line is: the manager has come up with a plan that would involve switching two of his people around. But the manager is worried that the boss won't buy the idea, so he is trying to lead the boss down a step-by-step path to the conclusion that he himself has reached. He also wants the boss to appreciate his ingenuity in arriving at the solution.

What could happen, however, is that the boss will run out of patience before the punchline is reached, especially if he is busy or distracted by other problems. He loses interest and will no longer be so receptive to what is actually a good idea.

If the manager were to take some cues from the sales rep, he would meet the "buyer resistance" he anticipates in a different way. He would know that when people on the receiving end can't figure out what they are being told (or "sold"), they become suspicious. If he repeats this kind of behavior, he may begin to encounter a very inattentive or resistant boss.

Of course, when people complain that others don't listen to them, there is always the unflattering possibility that they don't say anything worth listening to. There are times, however, when we all make it difficult for another person to listen to us, no matter how worthwhile our ideas. For example, say we catch someone on the run. He has a million other things on his mind, or he is already late for an appointment, or he is still mulling over the last conversation he had. And wham! We hit him hard with a whole new set of ideas. Who can blame him if he doesn't listen?

Sometimes, too, we can get so involved with telling stories in sequence, detailing steps A to B to C, that we lose sight of the need to get the message across clearly and speedily. In an effort to build suspense and to let the listener know, in endless detail, just how clever we were in handling every development, we put him or her to sleep.

A third self-imposed obstacle is neglecting to indicate to the listener just how our proposal will benefit him. For example, compare the following conversation openers:

You know, I was going through the accounts receivable depart-ment—I had to pick up a request form in distribution that hadn't been properly made out—and I happened to run into Jess Slade. And he said something interesting—we had been talking about . . . .

Hey, I just heard something in accounts receivable that should make you feel very happy.

There is surely no question in your mind as to which of these two "leads" would command greater attention.

Applying the rules

Let's go back to the earlier example of the manager who is telling his suspense story about Stanley and Edith and see how he might handle the transaction differently. Although he gets good marks for *knowing his product* (his solution to a work problem), what is of immediate interest is the benefit to the boss. A better opening line would be: "You know, I think I have a way to resolve all of those problems we've been having with the Scheduling group."

How's that for getting the boss's immediate interest?

To some extent, this manager *knows his prospect*, because he knows the benefit to the boss. But before he explains further, he needs to make sure that the boss is ready to listen. A simple question takes care of that. "Do you have a minute to discuss it?" Or, "Is this a convenient time to outline my suggestion?"

The next step is to *involve the boss*:

MANAGER: Edith doesn't seem happy with her job in scheduling. I think you're aware of that, aren't you?

BOSS: Yes, for some time now. (*Fine, the boss is getting involved.*)

MANAGER: One of the problems seems to be that Edith doesn't get along so well with some of those people there. I was trying to figure out how to handle that problem when I had another thought. Move her out of there. (*Pause.*)

BOSS: But who would we replace her with? (*Splendid. The boss is really into it.*)

MANAGER: With Stanley. He's had experience, and he gets along with those people. Doesn't it make sense? (*Trial close.*)

BOSS: Well, I'm not so sure.

So the manager explains further, emphasizing that Stanley has been complaining that he's not happy in Order Processing. And so on. Finally the manager asks for the order:

MANAGER: So it seems to me that we can put Edith on the correspondence desk. That would solve the friction between Edith and the others. And we can put Stanley back in what he wants to do. If you agree, I could have it set up within a week.

This step causes difficulty for a lot of people. They forget, or are too timid, to *ask for action*. But every argument should ask for something, even if only an answer to the question "Is this the way you see it?"

The boss is not ready to close. "What about Edith's assistant? I don't think she'll work with Stanley."

At this point, the manager listens, concedes that could be a problem, restates the original benefits—and asks for the boss's reactions and agreement.

Many people tend to react to resistance with an insistent "Yes, but . . ." The good salesperson listens, concedes that it is a problem (which it is in the buyer's mind), and considers the possibility that it might not be the real objection. For example, the boss might be reluctant to make any changes because he is about to go into the hospital, and he doesn't want people to know just yet.

This manager gets a high score for *being prepared to handle opposition*. He acknowledges that there could be a problem, at least in the boss's mind. Two common mistakes that people make when they encounter resistance are:

1. Denial of the objection

"That's no problem," a person says glibly, not reflecting on the damage done. The other person feels put down, as though his or her thinking has just been stamped deficient. It may not be a problem in your mind, but it may be in the other person's mind. Don't make the other person feel discounted by trying to deny the objection.

2. "Yes, but . . ."

This response is actually a less direct form of denial. Sellers who use this form of answer think they are being tactful. The first part of the answer may well be tactful ("Yes, I hear you . . ."), but the second part says, ". . . but you're wrong." Remember also that to respond directly to an objection, either with a "yes, but" or any other head-on approach, may waste time, because the objection may not be real.

To avoid these traps, I recommend the use of a "yes, and" approach. "Yes, I can see that you might regard that as a problem. There are some other considerations that you might want to take a look at. For example, these benefits." Acknowledge the negative, then turn positive.

The constructive approach is to concede the problem, then review the benefits and ask again for agreement. If the same objection is repeated, chances are it is real. In that case, *seek a commitment to buy if the objection is handled.* The manager would say, "As I understand it, you're reluctant to make the change because. . . . But if we can clear this up, how would you feel?" The boss thinks he might buy. The manager has the green light and says, "Okay, here's what we could do."

Chances are, the sale is made.

Now the manager asks for action again: "Shall I go ahead with it?" Suppose the boss still hesitates. You've asked for action and what you get is a stall. It's all too easy for a person to put off doing something, particularly if he hasn't heard enough to convince him he should act. Some suggested rejoinders:

BOSS: Maybe I should talk to Stanley about this.

MANAGER: Great! Why don't I see if Stanley can get together with us right now.

BOSS: Let me get back to you on this.

MANAGER: Fine. Why don't I summarize this in a memo to keep it fresh in your mind. I'll have it in your hands in an hour. Now when can we get together again?

BOSS: I'll have to think about this.

MANAGER: Sure. Is there anything in particular that is causing you to hesitate about making the decision now?

After you have said and done everything you can (including a follow-up memo), you may have to face facts. Your message hasn't gotten across. The only thing you can do then is to repeat it—and repeat it, and repeat it. But do so with all the good nature you can muster. After all, your objective is to get something from your boss—attention, a decision, approval for a project. If you set up a considerate schedule of repetition (don't camp on the boss's doorstep), chances are that, eventually, you will get the job done.

4

Developing a Persuasive State of Mind

Effectively influencing others consists of much more than practicing certain persuasive techniques. Although techniques are very important, there is a base on which these techniques must be built. This base consists of certain attitudes and behaviors that keep you in a persuasive mode. These attitudes and behaviors help establish your credibility with and acceptance by the people you deal with, and they work to make your persuasive techniques more effective.

Four key questions

Maintaining an awareness of what you want from, and what is happening in, a transaction is fundamental to successful persuasion. Gestalt therapy, founded by the late Fritz Perls, encourages behaviors that increase one's alertness to the here and now. Answering the following questions, which are derived from Perl's view of personal transactions, can help you develop and maintain *your awareness* of the purpose of the transaction, where it has been, and where it is going:

1. What do I want from this transaction?

Do you want information, help, an agreement, some form of action or commitment? You will have a specific objective in mind, in most cases, but you look for other results as well. For example, you want the satisfaction of presenting your story in a complete, honest manner and getting some favorable results from that presentation. You want your communication to be clear and acceptable. You would like acceptance by the other that you are a person who is pleasant and satisfying to work with. You would like to be admired and respected. Furthermore, you would like this to be the beginning, or the continuation, of a long and mutually beneficial relationship between yourself and the other.

2. What do I think the other person would like?

Obviously, your listener wants to spend time wisely and learn something from the conversation. The other person probably has a specific objective, too. He or she would like to get a good deal, and that can happen only if you provide the facts and the motivation to do "business" with you. The other person would like to feel that it is possible to rely on you and trust you. And, finally, the other person would like to feel that his or her professionalism, prestige, feeling of self-worth, and other needs have been enhanced by what is going on between the two of you.

3. What is going on at this moment?

It is important not to be so preoccupied with what you are saying and doing that you lose sight of the clues that the other person is giving. Is the other person interested, absorbed, following, thinking about what you are saying? Are you being as effective as you could be? Are you trying to relate to the listener? How can you get a reaction or some participation? Does the other have knowledge, opinions, or experience that you should try to tap at this point? If you don't have some idea of what is going on at all times with the other person and with yourself, then you are not in control of the situation. You both could be going nowhere.

*4. How does what is going on between us help us both
get what we want?*

If you want to lead to some kind of action, you must sense the
effectiveness of what is happening now. How does it contribute to
your both getting what you want? If you don't know that, the conversation may go off the track and never get back on course. To be
truly in control of the situation, you must be constantly aware that
what is happening at any given moment either contributes to the
desired course of action or leads away from it.

If your objective is to influence others—their thinking, their decisions, their actions—you must ask these questions of yourself—
and you must learn to do it automatically. If you do not really define
for yourself what you want from the interaction, then you will probably have to settle for whatever you get (and that may be what the
other person wants from you). Disciplining yourself to answer these
questions will help you to notice how the other person is reacting
and to pose questions or statements that will get the other person
involved.

In the transactions that you initiate, you are the persuader. It may
be that you want the other person to take on a difficult job, or come
around to your way of thinking on an important policy decision, or
join you on a project, or change the workflow procedures between
your two departments, or simply adopt your leisure plans. The point
is that you know where you want to go with this discussion. Unless
you give up your objective during it, then you must remain in
control. A continuing awareness of what is going on, here and now,
will help you do just that.

Maintaining control

When I described the concept of this book to a colleague, she said,
"Oh, it's really about control." Her response startled me. My first

reaction was to deny it, because the word "control" has negative connotations. But I came to realize that she was right. I am talking about control in the sense that a salesperson controls the sales interview, in the sense that the manager in Chapter 3 was in control because he knew where he wanted to go.

Controlling is not the same thing as dominating. Controlling a transaction means guiding it to a desired conclusion. When a person dominates a discussion, he or she is usually the only one who achieves genuine closure, a satisfaction often gained at the expense of others. The dominator has an agenda and an objective. What is most important is getting what he or she wants. Thus a dominator will force a decision, interrupt others, argue, manipulate, and push, either by position, authority, or overwhelming personality, everyone else along a predetermined direction.

By contrast, a good persuader knows the subject, knows how to present it and answer questions about it, knows how to get the other person involved in the presentation, and knows where the presentation should lead. Everything he or she says and does should be aimed toward achieving that objective. But the persuader also realizes that the other person needs to come out of the transaction with something. Therefore, that person is not only given a chance to interact but is encouraged to do so. The successful interview provides closure for both people. Both come out of it with at least some of their needs met.

The key word in my definition of control is *guiding*. Guiding is not pushing. The dominator pushes and forces, the controller guides. The person who initiates the transaction has a sense of where it should go. In a sales interview, which is our model, the salesperson works to keep the discussion on the track. When it strays, he finds a way to get it back. If the disruption is not serious and prolonged, the salesperson listens and replies, "That's very interesting," then resumes the presentation.

When the prospect strays far and wide, the salesperson listens carefully for a key word or a thought that might offer a bridge back to the sale. Here's an example: "I was especially interested in your comment about the high interest rate. It looks as if the cost of money is going to continue to be high, and that's why many of my customers appreciate the low cost of maintenance on this press. Let me take a moment to show you our average maintenance record over the past three years." Sometimes it is a precarious bridge, but it may hold.

There are times when the prospect seems impervious to bridging. In such a case, the salesperson calls attention to the off-track discussion but takes responsibility for it by saying, "Mr. Prospect, I'm beginning to be concerned that I'm taking more than I should of the time you have given me. I'd like to meet my obligations to you by giving you the rest of the information you need about our press. Unless you have all the facts, you can't possibly judge what a significant value this equipment represents for you." What the salesperson is selling at the moment is the notion that the prospect will benefit by ceasing to talk and by listening to the rest of the presentation.

The kind of controlling that a good persuader does is subtle. It sells the benefits to the listener, while letting the persuader proceed through the entire presentation, but always with respect for the other person, and always encouraging the participation of the other person. After all, using our sales interview analogy, the prospect is an equal partner in the transaction; nevertheless, he or she expects the salesperson to know how to conduct an interview that is informative, succinct, and purposeful.

When you're the unwitting buyer

One reason for maintaining control is that, if you lose it, you may become the "buyer" rather than the "seller." In other words, you end up buying the prospect's problems and reasons for not signing the order. This happens in many situations. For example, say you took your car to the garage for some repairs and emphasized how important it was to have the car back in two days. But when you show up, the service manager says, "Sorry. We'll have to keep it another day." You say, "But I told you I have to have it today. You agreed." He says, "I've had two men out with the flu. I couldn't anticipate that. I'm sorry, but. . . ."

If you accept his excuses, the service manager has just made a sale. You lost control. You hadn't intended to buy, but you did. You wanted your car, but instead you get a sad story. What the service manager was saying was, "I have a problem. Here, I want you to own it, too."

The same thing can happen at work. An employee can't seem to get to work on time. She says her babysitter comes to the house late. That is a problem for her, of course. But how about your problems? You want her at work on time.

A fellow volunteer on a township committee has offered to do some mimeographing. Several of you show up to get the forms and to distribute them. She hasn't done them. Her explanation is that her husband asked her to help entertain some clients. Your problem is that you have people wasting their time and forms that aren't getting distributed.

You walk into your boss's office to ask for a raise that you believe is deserved and overdue. She is very sympathetic, and then she tells you her problems. For one thing her budget has been cut for the last half of the year. Her requisition for hiring a new assistant has been denied temporarily. It's a sad story, especially for you. You went in with a problem; you emerge from the interview with hers. And no raise.

However, the more you are aware of what is going on, of others' attempts to influence you, the better prepared you are to buy only what you want to.

How do you resist these unwanted sales? Stay in control. Remember where you want the process to go. These people have simply assumed that you are going to accept their bill of goods, and they don't expect that you might refuse. They don't ask, "Is that all right with you?" or, "Will you please accept that?" No, they give you the presentation and expect the sale. But you don't have to give in, at least not before playing out your hand.

One way to resist the sale is to look at the person and listen. Then ask, "Yes?" You're indicating that you have heard but are not accepting the proposition. The burden is clearly on the other. The attempt to switch the burden to you has failed.

Probably the other person's response will be something like this: "Well, that's why I can't do such-and-such." Then you say, "I don't know that. What I'm hearing is that you have a problem. But so do I. You're apparently solving your problem. I'd like to solve mine."

You have now clearly indicated that you are not willing to buy. The next step is to decide jointly what can be done to solve your problem.

But what about the boss who gives you a sad story instead of a raise? Does this technique work there, too? Yes. There is no reason why you cannot say, "I can understand the pressures you're under. And I'm glad that you're sympathetic to my problem. I'm sure you'll agree with me that my performance this year has been very good. In fact, I've met and exceeded the goals we set. I'd like a raise, because I deserve it. What steps do you think we can take that will lead to my getting an increase?"

You're a tougher customer than the boss thought. And yet you are not offensive. You may not get the raise immediately; you may get a promise for one six months from now. Or you may hear something like, "Look, you have my okay to talk to the v.p. and present your case. He's the only one who could find the money."

Incidentally, in sales parlance, you were working for a "no." You pushed the discussion as far as you could, even if it meant not getting what you went in for. At least you gained some closure.

Some people signal their unwillingness to buy by responding, "That's your problem; that's not my problem." The wording is wretched, seemingly callous. But the idea behind it is sound. If I were to use that language, the implication is that I don't care about your problem. And there may be times when I shouldn't. But the problem to you is real and substantial. It may help things between us if I recognize that. However, my problem needs to be dealt with, and I don't want either of us to lose sight of that.

The essence of gaining and maintaining control is knowing where you want to go, and then gently but firmly keeping the interview or discussion on that track. It may not be easy, but it is the only way to get what you want.

Speaking forthrightly

The way you talk in your exchanges with other people is an important factor in your staying in control. The language you choose also presents an image of you. People judge you by it, and your words usually indicate how you feel about yourself. For example, look at these statements:

1. "I'm supposed to be in Chicago on Tuesday."
2. "I'll try to get it out by then, but I don't know."
3. "This came down from the top. I had nothing to do with it."
4. "Yeah, well, what really happened there, uh, is that, uh . . ."

The first sentence suggests that some person or external circumstances dictates where the speaker has to be on Tuesday. The second indicates doubt about ability and an avoidance of commitment. The third, of course, ducks all responsibility ("Don't blame me"). And the fourth expresses so much hesitation that the message loses impact and credibility. Many people habitually express themselves in these hesitant, tentative, passive terms.

Other people use language that conveys a quite different message: "I take responsibility for what I think, feel and say." For instance:

1. "Mr. Barton, I believe I ought to be reimbursed for this expense."
2. "I'll do everything I can to help you meet that deadline."
3. "This is the decision, and it is our job to carry it out."
4. "I'll see that the matter is taken care of first thing in the morning."
5. "Here's how the mix-up occurred."

The speakers are forthright. The language is specific, direct, and simple. The speakers commit themselves, saying in effect, "I'm in charge. I take responsibility. You can rely on me." Such language inspires confidence in other people and builds credibility.

Use active language, not passive. Accept responsibility, don't avoid. Present an image of confidence, not hesitancy.

Avoiding language barriers

When you use language that is tentative, uncertain, or flees responsibility, you create barriers to communicating. You can't do much persuading from behind a barrier. Remember that the first step in selling is to remove the barriers that exist between two people coming together and trying to talk to each other. Here are two such barriers you will want to avoid.

1. Intellectualizing

People intellectualize when they talk in abstract terms or make generalizations. For example, an interdepartmental meeting has been called to discuss the bidding for a contract. One manager says, "Of course, if we get this piece of business, we will be held to a tolerance of .009 inches. We have to think about that carefully."

It would be better if this manager were to say what he really means, perhaps, "Our plant record for staying within tolerances isn't anything we can brag about. I frankly worry about our being able to handle this job."

Such forthright talk might offend at first, but it will stand a better chance of getting the group to tackle the real issue than will the first, safer statement, which really doesn't indicate what they ought to be thinking about: achieving better quality.

Here's another example of intellectualizing: "This is a potentially high-risk venture" may simply mean "It scares me." People intellectualize either because they don't understand their own feelings or because they are afraid to reveal them.

2. *Neutralizing*

People neutralize their message and muffle their impact when they waltz around a subject, and they're particularly likely to do this when they know they will sound critical.

For example: "I really think that your most pressing problem at the moment, Frank, is hiring and maintaining ten salespeople in your region. Now, of course, the economy hasn't been that good. And I know that you've been awfully backed up on that special promotion deal. But I doubt whether we can hit our goals this year unless we can get those ten people, etc."

What this executive wants to say is, "Look, Frank, you were supposed to hire and train ten people. And you haven't."

Most people are brought up to be tactful, to avoid offending others. Neutralization throws up a lot of camouflage to conceal the harshness of reality. But the reality remains and, at some point, has to be dealt with.

Through intellectualization and neutralization, messages get blurred and lose their impact. Important things don't get done. Worse, people get the wrong messages and make mistakes. In the long run, people who intellectualize and neutralize frequently damage their credibility because other people think they are being evasive.

Here is a checklist to help you determine whether you are communicating clearly and directly or avoiding dealing with the other person in the transaction:

• Are you talking in general terms instead of asking specifically for what you want? A common example of this is the manager who sends out memos about cutting absenteeism rather than insisting that action be taken with individual offenders.

• Are you talking in terms of what ought to be rather than what is? Do you say, "We really have to get those ten people . . ." instead of, "We don't have ten people, and I'm upset that we don't."

• Are you sending mixed messages by saying one thing but looking another? Keeping a smile on your face when you are bursting with rage is a good example of a mixed message. Another common one is the boss who says he welcomes suggestions from subordinates and scowls every time an employee takes him up on it.

• Are you saying "you, we, one," to mask the truth: "*I* would like," "*I* want," "*I* think?"

• Are you looking at the carpet or over the other person's head while talking or listening?

These are the major clues that will warn you that you are muddling a necessary communication and, through embarrassment or fear, making it less effective—or even incomprehensible.

Projecting a positive image

A song Bing Crosby helped make famous offers good advice to people who want to be more influential: "You've got to accentuate the positive. . . ." Dr. Norman Vincent Peale became known for his theme: the power of positive thinking. No matter how hackneyed the phrase has become, it carries a strong and valid message. Professional salespeople bear this out. They are trained to "be assumptive," to believe that they will get the order. The salesperson does not walk into an interview wondering *whether* the prospect will buy but rather is concerned with *how* it will be done. No matter how rugged their sales interviews get sometimes, salespeople know that as long as they are in front of prospects they still have a shot at getting the order.

There is nothing Polyanna-ish about an experienced salesperson's positive attitude. It is a very pragmatic and essential attitude to have, one that is forged through years of frustration and failure and sparked by an increasing number of successes. These successes strengthen the salesperson's self-esteem and self-confidence and reinforce the conviction that he or she can and will do the job well. They've studied their successes and have learned how to repeat them.

Emulate this practice of analyzing successes and learning from them. Although it is possible to "learn from your mistakes," it is more constructive to analyze what you're good at—and why.

Having a positive attitude carries with it several advantages. For one thing, expecting a positive outcome gives you a certain freedom because you can be flexible in the way you achieve that outcome. You do not get locked into one particular scenario. Think back to a time when you were about to confront a friend or a colleague with a complaint. You might have listed for yourself all of your grievances and proof that you were correct in having them. What happened in your meeting? You probably didn't make the sale. You were so intent on getting all of your rehearsed points on the table that you didn't involve yourself sufficiently in what was happening between you and the other person. There was no dialogue. Instead two people gave speeches to each other. That is often the result of developing a negative scenario and then getting locked into it.

When you are thinking positively, you can say to yourself, "I'm going to make something good happen for me." Then you remain alert to whatever opportunities come your way to do just that. You open doors for yourself. You close them when you try to follow a negative scenario too closely.

Another advantage of being positive is that it permits you to direct your energies usefully, rather than arming for the wrong war. To illustrate, say you arrive back at your office after an unusually long lunch to find a handwritten note on your desk from your boss. She would like a word with you when you come in. What happens then? You are probably a bit nervous about having been away from the office so long, and you consider the possibility that the boss is going to comment on that. So you develop arguments in your mind to the effect that often you don't even go out to lunch, that sometimes in order to take care of business you postpone it or skip it altogether. Thus prepared you enter your boss's office to hear her say, "I wanted to let you know that I think your memo on the Houston branch office and your analysis of what's wrong down there are excellent."

A more profitable use of your energy would have been thinking about what you want to discuss with the boss. For instance, if you have been entertaining the idea of going to a trade convention in Florida, maybe you will get the chance to bring it up. Indeed, considering the pleasantness of her feedback on your memo, it would have been a great time to get her approval.

Being positive also makes a favorable impact on others. Watch the successful salesperson. Personal problems at home, an oncoming cold, disappointments from the last interview, these are all left outside the door of the next prospect's office. The principal reason the salesperson strives to be positive is to ensure the message is a clear one: I am here to persuade you that I have something of benefit to you. That message can too easily become contaminated by anger, worry, or disappointment that may be carried over from another occasion or transaction. The salesperson maintains a positive bearing sometimes under very trying circumstances. It takes a lot of work to put out positive messages.

Positive messages beget positive responses. Positive messages gain you the respect and trust of others. Unsure people often dwell on the negative. For example, inexperienced managers sometimes think they do their jobs by pointing out what is wrong with a work situation. But the professional manager or supervisor seeks to find what can be done to correct it. There's a vast difference between "won't work" and "can do." Most people prefer to be around people who can do. The person who dwells on what will work, what is right about this, rather than on what is not right, what won't work, broadcasts a self-confidence that inspires confidence in others.

The confidence of the positive person often makes good things happen for that person. When you put out the messages through your words, your expressions, your gestures, the tone of your voice, that this is the way you believe things should go, you'll often find others swinging around to your way of thinking. People, generally speaking, are much more agreeable to being influenced by the positive, confident person.

Utilizing negative scenarios

The previous paragraphs are not to discourage negative scenarios entirely. In fact, such scenarios can be useful. The prudent person develops a "What if . . ." scenario just in case it is needed. But there is a vast difference between making allowances for a possibility and actually expecting it to happen. Most negative scenarios do not get played out in reality. You can spend many hours anticipating what unpleasantries might occur between you and another person, but most times your fears are never realized. So not only did you waste your time, but your negative expectations probably hampered your effectiveness in dealing with others.

Be prepared for the "worst case"—but only so you can maintain a positive, confident attitude that will be reflected in your behavior. When you are approaching a challenging situation, follow these recommendations:

1. Develop your "what if" scenario

Go to the extreme: work up a worst possible case. That is, ask yourself to imagine what is the worst possible thing that could happen. For example, if you want to convince your boss that you are ready to move up to greater responsibility, that you have learned all there is to learn where you are, there are several possible responses your boss might make. He might agree with you. He might then suggest a move. On the other hand, he might not agree that you are ready. He could stall, saying, "Let me think this over." In the worst possible case, he might come back with, "I don't like having people work for me who are restless and bored. If you don't like what you are doing, find another job."

2. Analyze what you will do in each case

How would you handle opposition or a stall? (There will be specific recommendations on this for you in Chapter 7.) What recourse would you have if he threatened you, as in the worst case? For example, could you appeal somewhere else in the organization for more understanding and consideration?

3. Consider similar challenges of the past

How did you handle past challenges? What strengths were you able to bring to the situation that you might bring to this one? In short, review your previous successes and find out how you can apply their lessons now.

4. Know what you want to happen

The more clearly you define your goal, the better chance you have of reaching it—or of knowing when you have attained it. No matter what happens, never lose sight of your goal. If you are diverted, get back on the track. And if you don't get what you want immediately, don't give up until you know what is required for you to attain your objective. (Again, you'll get more specific advice on this in later chapters.)

Involving others

Good persuading involves both parties. The key word is *involvement*. When you seek to involve others, to encourage them to express their needs and wants, to give you feedback on what you are doing in the interaction, you convey a message of respect for the other people. You exhibit a win-win mentality rather than a win-lose. Let us both get something out of this, you say. The salesperson who approaches a prospect as someone who is meant to be beaten has often lost the contest before it has begun. Such a salesperson is tempted to be condescending, pushy, and insensitive. He deserves to lose the sale.

And that is true of the manager. The idea that the boss's is the only voice that counts doesn't work these days. Today's manager must be more of a coordinator and developer than a dictator. Nothing will do a manager in faster than displaying the attitude, "I get what I want regardless of what others want," or, even worse, "I get what I want any way I can."

Here are a few of the ways that skillful salespeople demonstrate that they respect their prospects. Managers, take note.

Accept opinions

They are careful to avoid even seeming to put down the prospect's response. For example, a good salesperson always uses the "yes, and" approach rather than the "yes, but." The latter says, "Your statement doesn't hold water, and I'll show you what I mean." The former says, "I understand that you feel that is a consideration, and I would like to add another one." However full of holes another person's comments might be, assume that that person takes them seriously and act accordingly. The worst thing you can do in an exchange with an employee, another manager, or anyone else, is to make him feel wrong or foolish.

Accept feelings

In any human interaction, feelings come into play. There may be anger, joy, suspicion, impatience, mistrust, etc. If the prospect is suspicious or shows a lack of trust, the salesperson accepts the feeling even if he or she doesn't see a reason for it. When you accept the fact that another person feels a certain way, you are not necessarily agreeing with those feelings. You are not saying, "If I were in your place, I would feel that way, too." You are simply acknowledging that the other person feels a certain way. If you wish to overcome negative feelings in another, do as the salesperson does: give more reasons to buy, more benefits of buying. Don't waste time trying to argue the person out of those feelings. Extend to the other the same privilege you claim for yourself. You have a right to your feelings. So does the other person.

Avoid labels

When a salesperson meets an obstacle, he wouldn't dream of saying to the prospect, "You're fighting this," or asking, "Why are you so stubborn?" Or if a prospect raised her voice, the salesperson wouldn't say, "I didn't mean to make you angry." Putting labels on behaviors is risky. If the other person resists the label, then you are debating who is right instead of discussing matters of substance. Remember that each of us is an expert in our own feelings. If you want to call attention to the other's feelings or behavior, do so through acknowledging your perceptions: "I sense that something I've said has disturbed you." (Or more simply, "Have I upset you?") In that way, you put your perceptions on the line rather than the other's behavior. The other's response will be less defensive.

Take responsibility for misunderstanding

If the prospect shows that he doesn't fully understand a point, or if he gives a response that is off the track, the salesperson is careful not to say, "You're wrong," or "You didn't understand me." The salesperson takes responsibility for the error. "I'm sorry, I guess I didn't make that as clear as I should have."

In some interactions where there is less than perfect understanding, you'll hear one person complain, "You didn't listen to me." That may or may not be true. What could be true is that the speaker didn't say what he or she means to say. When there's misunderstanding or failure in communication, the smart person accepts responsibility, repeats or rephrases, and stays on the track. It's a generous gesture that pays off in the other person's increased good will.

Look for options

The salesperson walks into an interview thinking, "I want this order," but also realizing that there is no one best way to get it. The effective salesperson is aware of options in nearly every situation. The salesperson and the prospect develop various avenues along which the dialogue can travel. The prospect may come up with a benefit that the salesperson has not defined. The sales representative identifies an application for the product and service that surprises and pleases the prospect. That is one of the things that makes selling so fascinating: there is no one way to sell.

Every dialogue is different; every dialogue generates options. Hmm, you might say as you listen, that's something I hadn't thought of; it has possibilities. Options are things to say, actions to take, directions to follow. Being open to them, becoming aware of them, defines the selling mentality. And it provides you with a lot of room to move about in.

When I walk around my organization, I make a point of talking with people. I want information, clarification, help, favors, etc. Other people want the same from me. But only mutual respect will create a successful interaction now and a satisfying, rewarding relationship over the long term. Respect for the other person is essential for influence and persuasion. You demonstrate it in your behavior toward others. It can be feigned, but not for long.

5

Practicing the Fine Points of Persuasion

Your opportunities to influence others arise constantly throughout the day. Many of these interactions are spontaneous or initiated by others. You do not have time to develop a presentation or prepare for opposition. Nevertheless, you want to make an impact. You may want to cement cooperation, strengthen understanding of a proposal, obtain some information, gain a favor, enhance your image as a useful resource, obtain sponsorship for an idea, enlist an ally. The list is endless.

It is important to bear in mind that even seemingly casual inter-actions can accomplish something for you. Although you may not have the chance to prepare for each interaction, you can practice certain selling skills so that you automatically put them to work whenever the opportunity arises. You can sharpen the finer points of persuasion.

First, you must have the intention of being persuasive. This is part of the attitudinal base we talked about in the previous chapter. Being effective in dealing with other people depends in large part upon your alertness to your objective and your positive attitude about achieving it.

Your success in influencing other people also depends on your awareness that those others have needs and wants. You may not always know specifically what those needs and wants are, but you know that they exist and that you must make an effort to satisfy them. You cannot hope to meet others' needs and wants or to use their strengths unless you routinely involve them in the transaction. They must feel as if they are partners in whatever is going on. It is not enough for you to assert yourself. You must be responsive and sensitive to the other people in the transactions that you enter into.

Assertiveness-responsiveness

A helpful description of what I am talking about is provided by consultant Malcolm E. Shaw in his book, *Assertive-Responsive Management* (Reading, MA: Addison-Wesley). Shaw identifies these behaviors in interacting with others: aggressive, nonassertive, assertive, responsive, and assertive-responsive.

As an example of *aggressive* behavior, here is one supervisor talking to another:

I'm still waiting for that batch you were supposed to send over an hour ago. You asked me to give it special attention, and I cleared the line. Now what? I've got these people sitting around waiting for you. You've done this to me, you've put me out, and when I call you down on it, you always have some excuse. Well, I want you to know that I'm not giving you any special attention, and you can keep your excuses to yourself.

There's no question that this supervisor has expressed himself. But he is unloading on his colleague. His words express an "I'm-OK-but-you're-not" attitude. He puts the other supervisor down. He wants to win, and he makes sure that the other person loses. And how will the other supervisor feel? Resentful at least. Communication and cooperation between these two will be hard to find for some time.

The domineering person may often encourage nonassertive behavior in others. People who are nonassertive usually want to escape conflict. I once knew a manager who was uncommonly quarrelsome and obnoxious. In staff meetings he dictated to everyone present. He raised his voice, laughed at people who offered opposing views, and told them they were very naive or inexperienced. In a very short time most of the people around the room fell silent, staring at the table or at one another, avoiding any eye contact with the boss. The boss's aggressive behavior evoked nonassertiveness in his subordinates.

Not surprisingly, this kind of manager will pay dearly for the nonassertiveness he craves. The resentment of subordinates over being bullied and put down will come to the surface in various ways. People will not keep him informed of departmental matters that he should know about. They will gossip and laugh at him behind his back. The work done will frequently be enough to meet basic standards but no more.

Assertive behavior is characterized by giving information and expressing wants. For example, the supervisor in the opening example could have said:

I'm still waiting for that batch you said you would send over an hour ago. You asked me to give it special attention, and I cleared the line. Your delay in sending it has caused me inconvenience and cost the company money. If you don't send the batch now, I'll have to put the line to work on something else."

There's little question that the manager is unhappy. But he is straightforward and expresses no judgments or putdowns.

This supervisor would be judged *responsive* if, instead of conveying his wants, he pointed out that the line was shut down, and asked whether there was a problem. If he is upset, he doesn't show it. Responsive behavior is seen in people who seek out the opinions or wishes of others without asserting their own.

It is possible to be assertive *and* responsive. Here is how Shaw describes assertive-responsive behavior: ". . . each of the parties must . . . assert a position, put out information, and perhaps engage in selling or convincing others as to the rectitude of their stance. Conversely, each of the parties . . . must be willing to listen, to draw out, and to be Responsive and open to the view of others." Each makes a point but listens to the other.

Let's go back to the assertive supervisor. "I'm still waiting for that batch . . . Your delay . . . cost the company money. You must be having some sort of problem. Obviously I have a problem. What can we do to solve both of our problems?" The message is clear: "We share a problem; let's both work on the solution. You are probably concerned, as I am. I have resources; so do you. Let's put them together." Those are the messages that are given out in the assertive-responsive approach.

The assertive-responsive mode is especially valid in managing people. Many managers insist on aggressiveness: "This analysis is incomplete. You must have tried to get it done at the last minute. It just shows me that you take a careless approach to your job, almost as if you don't care."

The assertive approach: "This analysis falls short of what I wanted. The data are incomplete. I can't accept this. Please do it over."

Then you add responsiveness: "I can't accept this. I'm disappointed, and I doubt whether you are happy with it. Let's talk about how you can produce the kind of analysis that would satisfy us both."

When you are assertive-responsive, you intend to communicate, to share, to give information. You want to express your wants. You know that the other person has wants. You don't want to put the other person down. You discuss feelings. You have eye contact which is comfortable for both of you. Your facial expressions and other nonverbal gestures match your feelings and the words you use.

It isn't easy for most people to be assertive-responsive in their interactions with others. A large number of people tend to be nonassertive or very responsive, and neither approach leads to persuasiveness. Other would-be persuasive people are dominant types, strongly ego-centered.

In everyday transactions, there is a basic form of involvement:

"How are you?" Many people these days make fun of the question, labeling it as meaningless. But it is an attempt to open the door of interaction, to say, "This is your chance to say what you wish. I'm listening." The principle is to ask questions. Anything that will encourage the other person to open up and talk about what you want him or her to discuss is assertive-responsive behavior. For example, if you have made a suggestion, or advanced an idea, some of the questions you might ask are:

- "Does what I am saying make sense to you?"
- "I'm especially interested in how you see the consumer survey proposal."
- "What's your reaction overall?"
- "I sense that you have a problem with the three-week deadline."
- "This seems to be in line with some of the ideas that you've expressed during the meeting. Am I correct?"

Watch the other person's reactions. Listen to the words. Find ways to check things out. The message that you want to convey is, "Here is the issue. Let's work it out together."

Watch the I's

Ego-centered people can easily be identified by their excessive use of the word I. They may even give the impression that there is little room in the universe for anyone else. "This is the way I want it done," the I-centered manager orders. (Never mind what *you* want.)

Look at the effect of the use of "I" in the following letter:

I want to thank you for your note of the 13th. I'm certainly pleased that you found our arrangements satisfactory. I look forward to seeing you again in the near future.

The sameness is boring. The following could be substituted:

Your note of the 13th was very welcome. I'm certainly pleased that you found our arrangements satisfactory. Let's get together again in the near future.

The use of "I" can be repetitive and obnoxious. People are constantly made aware of the overbearing presence of the speaker or writer. After a time, people become uneasy, wondering if the speaker or writer can actually admit to an equal relationship or be genuinely concerned with others.

The ego-centered manager presents a similar problem. Employees wonder how much credit they will get while working for such a person. For example, I once knew a manager who took credit for nearly every major development or decision in his 30-year history with his company, as well as for every good thing that happened in his department. Even though some of his employees were performing in a superior fashion, that was, in his opinion, a function of his wisdom and training. There was, to say the least, much disaffection among employees in that department.

The ego-centered person risks losing the respect and trust of others. The person who is aggressive or assertive much of the time probably gains short-term objectives and immediate rewards. But over time, the good will and cooperation of others fade, even when they are subordinates. You don't have to spend much time in an egotist's department to pick up the resentment, the lowered commitment, the passive resistance that will probably eventually hurt the manager's reputation and progress.

Good salespeople know that seldom do they get a sale by pushing and pressuring, by assaulting the barriers that a prospect puts up. Their sales come when they involve the prospect, actually making the prospect a participant in the process.

Little success derives from solitary effort. How many of your own achievements did you accomplish without the actual help, encouragement, guidance, and sponsorship of others? While it's true that most highly successful people, including salespeople, lean strongly in the direction of being ego-centered, they usually know how to mute that fact, to compensate for it. They know the monologue is not an effective persuasion technique. They know that the genuine rewards come from involving others in their efforts to attain their own goals.

These then are the characteristics of assertive-responsive behavior:

- You assert your needs or wants;
- You express how you feel (hopeful, angry, disappointed, curious, etc.);
- You enlist the aid or participation of the other;
- You look for a solution or answer.

Listening

Few human acts denote as much respect and consideration for the other person as does listening well. Here are three recommendations to enhance the impact that your listening makes on the other person:

1. *Maintain eye contact*

Maintaining eye contact is not easy to do. In fact, most people require training in it, but it is very important to learn. Have you talked with someone and watched him or her frequently look away, over your shoulder, or down at something on the desk? It probably made you feel that what you were saying was not of much interest, that in fact you were not of importance to the other person. When you maintain eye contact throughout a discussion, you not only convey respect for what the other person is saying, but enhance the probability that you will get more respectful attention when you talk.

2. *Don't interrupt*

You have undoubtedly found yourself talking to another person who couldn't wait until you finished to speak. This person doesn't seem to listen to your words. He's looking for a cue to speak himself. He watches for a break in your conversation. You take it as a put-down.

Give the other person ample time to express himself. Don't try to complete sentences that the other person is slow to finish. When you try to guess what the other person is saying, you create resentment, slow the process down, and generally obscure the direction that the conversation is taking.

3. *Provide closure*

People need to close out a subject. Watch what happens in this scenario:

YOU: Those are the reasons why I thought that, if we changed the reporting date to the second week of the month, we might be able to save some employee time.

OTHER: Yeah. Oh, by the way, before I forget, there's a meeting of the task force Wednesday morning. I was told to tell you.

Wouldn't it have been nice if the other person had responded to your proposal and then told you about the meeting? "Yeah, let's do it. It's a good idea. Oh, by the way . . . " When people are not permitted to close out a subject, when others switch to a different track abruptly, the speakers can't be blamed for thinking that the others haven't listened.

Use your voice effectively

Experts in communication say that younger people, having been raised on television, are accustomed to noise. They think nothing, apparently, of creating even more of it. If you're in a restaurant, a bus, any public place frequented by young people in their teens or 20s, one thing you'll notice is that they tend to talk loud.

Talking loud is widely interpreted as stemming from immaturity, insensitivity, or exhibitionism. None of these labels is positive. Talking loud does not enhance the persuasiveness. Be aware of the volume at which you conduct a conversation. A loud voice at the least distracts the listener, and at most it turns the other person off.

Practice speaking in a low register. Many accomplished conversationalists and executives have become skilled at keeping their voices out of the higher register where it may grate or sound less authoritative. I was once in a meeting where one executive spoke slowly, carefully, in a well-modulated voice in a lower register. He made a tremendous impact, although I wasn't sure that he had said anything of substance. Style is no substitute for substance, but style can make an impact, especially when it is tied to substance.

The power of pauses

Speaking fast can enhance credibility, but the same speed can get very tiresome. Vary your speed, and make use of pauses.

Pauses can serve several purposes. For example:

The pause to get agreement

In writing, the important points are set off in paragraphs. In speech, you can do the same thing with pauses, providing time for a point to hit home. For example: "John, Mary is out sick, as you know, and the assignment has to be finished by tomorrow (*pause*) . . . so that means someone else will have to take over." In certain situations, you may not even have to finish the sentence yourself. The other person will do it for you, agreeing instantly with what you already know.

The pause for calm

If someone reacts emotionally to something you have said or done, a quick-on-the-trigger rebuttal from you will not have a calming effect. But a stretch of silence could help that person to hear his or her words and provide the chance to reevaluate the tone of those remarks—and perhaps reconsider the remarks themselves.

The pause to recapture attention

If you have been speaking too much and too fast and the other person's mind is obviously wandering, pause. Sit calmly. Gaze intently. When your eyes meet once more, you can continue the conversation. The other person may even apologize for the lack of attention.

The pause to impress

The chief executive officer wants to know if you can get a report out by Thursday. A quick "Of course!" will not be as reassuring as a reply such as: "Well, there is that all-day Wednesday meeting, and my own secretary will be on vacation all week, but (*pause*) . . . I'm quite sure I can get it to you by then."

Keeping your face and posture relaxed plays a large part in the effective use of the pause. Even an unplanned pause—when you're caught by surprise and at a momentary loss for words—can be turned to good effect if you immediately react by relaxing instead of betraying your discomfort with signs of tension.

Gestures

It is difficult to speak definitively about the messages we convey with our gestures. The science of nonverbal communication is not yet, in my opinion, as scientific as its proponents claim. But there is no question about the ability of gestures to enhance or detract from the spoken word. A few pointers are in order:

1. Avoid expansive or exaggerated gestures

Grand gestures distract. Some broad gestures are viewed as very childlike, which is hardly the image you'd like to create.

2. Match your gestures to the spoken message

Obviously the gesture should add to the message, not take away from it. Make an effort to become conscious of what you are expressing with your hands and the rest of your body. In most cases, the best gestures are those that you have developed naturally, without thinking of them, as long as they do not carry vestiges of child-hood or adolescent habits. Just as you work to increase the impact of your language, you should study to improve the impression that your gestures make.

3. Be wary of touching

Some people are touchers. They like to touch other people's arms and shoulders while they talk to them. Touching increases intimacy, and some people like it. Others are threatened or repelled by it. You take a chance when you touch others' bodies without knowing whether they are comfortable with it.

4. Use gestures in moderation

There are people about whom it is said that if you tie their hands, they can't talk. But their gesturing hands don't necessarily communicate, either. Hands and arms that are constantly moving are distracting.

5. Watch your body language when listening

Many people would be appalled to know how much their faces reveal of their feelings and reactions when they listen. Their expressions register disbelief, disgust, impatience, distrust—or at least they are perceived that way by the listener. Try also to avoid the I-dare-you-to-persuade-me stance: arms crossed, chin on chest, face screwed up in a scowl. Some people get upset even when their listeners do no more than cross their arms. If you want to convey interest, smile, nod, or listen impassively.

Word barriers

Match your words to your message. Choose words that say exactly what you mean and that will be understood by your listeners. Ill-chosen words are a sure barrier to communication. Your listener sits there distracted or annoyed by something you have said, while you continue to talk, unaware that the prospect is no longer paying attention, having failed to surmount the verbal barrier you have built.

It takes continuing alertness to avoid those barriers. Some recommendations for keeping your language easy for listeners to follow:

1. Watch the jargon

Many of the graduate students I encounter in my field, organizational behavior, seemingly cannot speak English. They communicate in jargon, and that is most irritating to someone who doesn't know the language. Jargon is fine for insiders because it can be a form of shorthand. But to outsiders, jargon can be impenetrable and infuriating.

2. Use words that are common and universally understood

You may have an excellent vocabulary, but you are selling a product or idea, not demonstrating your expertise with words. Unwittingly, you may have let some large, "impressive" words and jargon creep into your speech. Get back to clear words of one or two syllables. That still leaves you a wide variety, and they are safer to use. You cannot afford to distract your listener from the importance of what you are saying with a word or phrase he might not understand.

3. Cleanse your talk of words that don't mean much

All of us fall into speech habits that are annoying or bothersome to others. A good example are the parenthetical expressions, "You know . . ." or, "I mean . . ." Some people distract their listeners with these snags every few words. Even using them every sentence or two can impede the impact of your message.

4. Know how words are pronounced, and use common pronunciations

You characterize, for example, someone as "seCREtive." Some people learned this as the preferred pronunciation. However, most people say SECretive. The first pronunciation may work, but you're liable to wind up with a puzzled listener who has to take a few seconds to figure out what you just said—seconds during which your other words aren't heard. So stick with the pronunciations that most people are comfortable with.

5. *Follow the rules of usage*

Many people say infer, when they mean imply. The listener infers (understands or interprets), the speaker implies (suggests). No one is annoyed by hearing someone consistently use the language correctly. But there are at least some people who will be irritated with you if they think you don't know how to handle English properly. (A useful, and very slim, volume on the proper use of English is *The Elements of Style*, by William Strunk, Jr. and E. B. White [Macmillan].)

Using humor

Joking with another person can be a risky business. Some people will catch the joke, others will not. Those who don't may feel sheepish. If they suspect that the humor is directed against them, they will be annoyed or angry. My experience is that no more than half the people you tell a funny remark to will catch on. The other half, as I've indicated, will have varying reactions.

Anytime you use humor, remember that many listeners will not get it, especially if it is dry or subtle humor (which is why some stand-up comedians laugh at their own jokes as a signal to the audience).

Your use of humor may not quite suit you, and that will lessen its impact on others. For example, picture a staff meeting where one executive arrives late, looking embarrassed. The manager in charge makes a joke about the tardiness and everyone laughs, including the latecomer. In another group, a different manager may make the same joke. This time the laughs seem forced and people look down at the table. This time the humor does not suit the would-be humorist.

A sense of humor can make quite a positive impact on co-workers. But when the impact is negative, what has gone wrong? It's not necessarily in the remark but in the person making it. Some executives simply should not try to use humor that seems even remotely to be a comment on other people. These questions might give you some clues as to whether you can have the humorous effect you want:

Are you uneasy when a co-worker makes even a mild joke at your expense?

If you would prefer that people not make even a gentle joke about you, then trying to make funny remarks about other people's foibles is not a good idea. You'll come across as believing that you are sacrosanct but others are fair game. Other people are less likely to take offense at your jokes at their expense if they know that you're the first to take a pin to your own balloon.

Do you tell stories that put yourself in a less-than-perfect light?

A sense of humor has to be properly pointed, and inward is better than outward. The manager who laughs at himself or includes himself in the joke is better off than the one who makes fun of others.

Do people seem to feel comfortable in joking with you?

If people never rib you, or do it seldom, take it as an indication that they don't feel you take humor about yourself very well. In that case, it's wise to resist the temptation to kid other people.

When the atmosphere is right and people understand that there is room for give-and-take, then humor can play a useful role in reducing tensions and encouraging feedback. But when executives are not seen taking jokes as well as giving them, their use of ribbing comments may increase tension and even seem to mask ill-feeling.

Key words

In short, practice to make your messages:

* Interesting to hear;
* Valuable to accept;
* Easy to understand and to act upon.

But no matter how skillfully you speak or write, you must be:

Authentic

Your manner of communicating must be perceived as consistent with the real you. You don't have to reveal everything about yourself, but what you choose to reveal should be genuine.

Credible

A word to couple with this one is authoritative. Credibility and authority are the cornerstones on which all selling is based. I won't listen to you carefully if I wonder whether I can trust you. Credibility takes a long time to build. But once your listeners believe that you can be trusted, and further, that you know what you are talking about, you are well on your way to being persuasive.

Respectful

By giving respect to others, you get it from them in return. But it is also very important that you respect yourself. No one can command or expect respect without first granting it to himself or herself.

Your behavior should say, "I take myself seriously. What I have to say is important." The check against taking oneself too seriously is to show clearly that you regard others quite seriously as well.

6

Selling Yourself and Your Ideas

Most ambitious and successful people want to create and take advantage of opportunities. Other people seem to take events as they occur; they seem content to let things happen to them and let others control what comes their way. They see no reason to try to become more influential or persuasive. At best, they do not often get their way; at worst, they become victims.

The contrast between these two types of people was made very clear to me in the case of a manager I have known for a number of years. Bill held a responsible editorial position in a rather large publisher of magazines. Here's how he described his situation: "I had been with the company for a number of years. I was well-known in the organization, and, as far as I knew, well thought of. The job was great. The money was good, and I had, or at least believed I had, a fair degree of job security."

But he didn't take the job and the security for granted. There were disturbing signs that the situation that had existed for many years might not continue indefinitely. For example, the circulation on Bill's magazine had fallen consistently over the years. Some of Bill's associates grumbled about the rotten job that the circulation department was doing, but he wasn't sure that that was where the blame should be directed. "I felt that we were fat and happy. Maybe too fat and too happy. We weren't the cutting edge of our field as we should have been. We had been once."

There was a sameness about the articles in the magazine. The excitement had gone out of the copy. New developments were played down or ignored. Quality had dipped. Now and then Bill would hear disparaging comments about his publication from editors in other divisions of the company.

One problem that Bill faced personally was the conflict that had developed between his boss (the editor) and him. Bill was frequently overruled in his decisions on which articles to run or which to rewrite drastically. "There was a time," Bill recalls, "when my boss wanted to have the best magazine in the company. But he'd lost that. He had reached a dead end. He knew that he wouldn't go any further in the company, and he was very bitter about it."

Bill believed the whole department was suffering as a result of his manager's malaise. "I decided that I didn't want to be known as his boy. If the ship went down, I sure wasn't going to be there on the bridge with him." Bill began to expand his lines of communication, to maintain closer contact with what was happening outside his division. He strengthened his acquaintance with other influential managers and editors in the company. He came up with new product ideas—"Anything that would justify my sitting down with higher management."

Bill knew that his boss did not get along very well with *his* boss, the executive vice-president of the organization. So Bill looked for opportunities to show his friendliness toward the officer. "Whenever I saw him, I'd greet him with a smile. I usually had a question to ask or an opinion that would give us a chance to talk. I wanted him to know that I didn't share my boss's dislike for him."

Thanks to Bill's cultivated sources of information, the news came that an editor of another of the company's publications was planning to take an early retirement. "I sent the executive v.p. a confidential note suggesting an appointment with him. I told him that I had been thinking about my future, and that I wanted to see how some of my plans might fit in with the direction the company was taking." The older man invited him to lunch. Bill prepared for the meeting by talking discreetly with co-workers who knew the v.p. better than he did. He wanted to know more about the man he would be dealing with. Over the meal Bill gave him an informal presentation. "I had it all organized in my mind. I told him I wanted a change, that I had a lot to offer and that I wanted a position that would give me more freedom to operate. He knew exactly what I meant." Bill listed his strengths, his experience, his knowledge, his management credentials. "He knew that I had been working under some very difficult conditions."

Bill was also very specific about what he needed. He knew that he was qualified to take over the editorship of a magazine, on the same level as his boss. He didn't reveal that he knew about the rumored retirement. The v.p. listened carefully, showed that he agreed with Bill's assessment of himself, and suggested that there might be a position opening up. "He told me to be patient, that the company definitely wanted me to stay with them, that there were a number of decisions that were being made, some of which would affect me."

Bill didn't have to wait very long. First came the announcement that his magazine was being folded, that decreasing circulation and advertising revenues had made the magazine a marginally profitable operation at most. The magazine would be continued for one year, then cease publication.

Bill's boss, the editor, was very bitter, as were many of Bill's editorial colleagues. The boss was transferred to another division to a job that everyone recognized would keep him out of the way. Bill was promoted to editor. He was also assured that if he was successful at nursing his dying publication through its last months, he would be given another job in the company. Bill was one of the few people in his department to be retained. Most of the editors were told that they would be out of a job at the end of the twelve months.

After publication of the magazine was suspended, Bill was announced as the replacement for the retiring editor, the position that Bill had sold himself for. "Most of my colleagues were out on the street. They were very angry. And I can understand that. Some of them had been with the company for years. They had apparently assumed that they would be there until they retired."

Bill's example provides a vivid contrast between the person who takes initiative, exercises control, makes things happen, and the person who takes whatever comes. Bill sold effectively. He knew his product. He knew his prospect, and that he would be receptive to Bill's presentation. He anticipated his prospect's needs. It was a good match: the benefits that Bill offered would soon be needed by the v.p.

Notice that Bill did his selling over a period of time, not just at lunch with the senior man. There was an extensive pre-presentation period during which Bill worked to gain better visibility, to establish his image as a person to be considered seriously. Once he had decided that he wanted to make a change, he began to involve his prospect at every opportunity. Finally he was ready to make his presentation and ask for action. He was also ready to meet opposition. "I had a good idea of my weaknesses. I decided before lunch that I was going to acknowledge them and emphasize the pluses I could bring to the job. I wasn't going to spend any time trying to explain away the minuses."

Selling a radical change

The following case history shows that you can take what many people may regard as an implausible proposition and sell it. For twelve years I made my living as a salesman, first selling group insurance and then selling the products of The Research Institute of America, a large business advisory organization that, through newsletters and membership programs, alerts executives to various problems and opportunities such as government programs, court decisions, labor relations, and market trends.

Even though I had been a successful salesman, I wanted to be a professional writer. For some eight years, I had been getting up around five o'clock each morning to work on a novel before going to my sales appointments. I produced four manuscripts, none of which was published. Nevertheless, my desire to have a career as a writer became stronger.

One possible career move became very clear to me. The Institute's professional staff did a great deal of writing in preparing the various reports that RIA sent out to its members and subscribers. My chief problem, I had been told in response to my tentative inquiries about the possibility of switching from the field to the professional staff, was that I just didn't have the proper credentials to be considered an expert.

But there came a time when I was desperate to make the switch, and by then I was convinced that I did in fact have something to sell. I made an appointment with the vice president in charge of sales, a man I had come to know and like. I also knew that he would give me a hearing. My presentation lasted ten or eleven minutes. I made the following points:

1. I suspected that the Institute was about to expand its professional staff (business was on the upswing; I was guessing about the expansion). They would need new people, and I wanted to be considered for a position.

2. I had an unusual combination of talents and knowledge. I was a successful, experienced salesman who knew how to write about sales and marketing.

3. I knew the Institute's products and marketing. That would give me a strength not shared by the other professionals who knew much less about how RIA sold its products. I knew the Institute's audience since I had been selling to them for nearly five years. I also made the point that I had sold to top management for all of the twelve years I had been in sales, so I really knew a great deal about their problems and needs.

I had limited credibility. They knew about my selling, but had no way of knowing about my writing ability or whether I could work in an office with other writers and editors.

The v.p. arranged for me to have an interview with a manager on the professional staff. The interview was rather perfunctory. I was asked whether I would be willing to write a sample article for an Institute publication. Of course, I was very willing. (I later discovered that this was intended to be the knockout blow.)

As it turned out, fortunately, I was also very capable. The discipline and practice of writing fiction all of those mornings proved to be good for my writing skills. Furthermore, I had always had a practice of analyzing sales situations and selling because the whole process fascinated me. So my analytical skills, which no good writer or editor can afford to be without, were in top working order.

After a lengthy interviewing and writing process, I joined the professional staff. My success in making the switch was a combination of good timing and planning. They were going to expand the staff, as I had guessed. I had built enough credibility and respect that I had to be listened to. My presentation, as it turned out, was on target. Initially, there was a great deal of opposition. The interviewing manager's biases were evident to me from the outset. But I disarmed him by saying, in effect, "Look, you don't have to risk anything but a little of your time. Give me a chance to prove that I can be of benefit to you and the staff. That's all I ask."

It is a good approach, especially when your sales proposition is unusual or radical.

Selling your own product

When you attempt to sell yourself or your ideas, you're experiencing a situation that is somewhat different from what most salespeople encounter. You have a personal investment in the product. If you are turned down, you can hardly be blamed for taking it personally to some extent. Someone who sells autos or insurance or computers learns very soon not to take most turndowns personally.

When you mount a campaign to sell yourself, as an individual or your own ideas, you have to take certain factors into consideration that you might not have to if you were selling something else. You may also want to take extra precautions, especially in the planning.

The most vulnerable time in the sale of an idea is the initial stages. If you try to sell an idea that still has holes in it, it goes down the tube (and part of you, perhaps, goes with it). An idea needs to be fully developed if it is to be seriously considered. An opinion or a suggestion is just the starting point.

To help you shape the idea to make it salable, take these steps:

1. Define the problems the idea will solve

In Bill's case, the message was twofold: one, the company will need to fill an opening, and two, you are not using my skills well in my present job but they qualify me perfectly for the opening. That's it. Here is the problem; here is the solution.

2. Define the opportunities the idea will create

While identifying problems is important, it's even more important to translate your ideas into opportunities. Sometimes you may wish to dwell only on the opportunities in your presentation. For example, if your boss is retiring or being promoted, and if you want to be considered as a successor, you would scarcely want to point out your boss's deficiencies that you intend to correct.

3. List the trade-offs that may have to be made

What advantages of the existing system will have to be sacrificed in order to gain the greater good incorporated in the idea? Why are the trade-offs worth the trouble? The costs? When I applied for the staff position, I realized that they could probably have hired a younger man from outside with a more demonstrated writing ability for less money. Yet I brought a knowledge of Institute practices and products to the job that an outsider wouldn't have. It was the trade-off they were willing to make.

4. Decide on the best way to channel the idea

Who are the influential people the proposal must reach? Who is the first person to contact? Which people can be counted on for support, and what is the best way to enlist their support?

In selling, much emphasis is placed on getting to the right person, the one who has the authority to buy. When you're selling yourself, you need to go to the person in the organization who can buy. Generally you would go through your boss, not over his or her head. But the point is, you'd like to do the selling to the person who makes the decision. Don't waste your time giving presentations to people without authority unless they can help you to make the sale, or unless they can at least lend moral support. If these people have influence with the decision-maker, sell them just as hard.

5. Choose a vehicle

Big ideas are not of the usual suggestion-box variety. It may take a detailed position paper, or a real sales promotion, or both, to communicate your idea properly. An estimate of costs is usually a must.

But don't substitute pieces of paper for you. Use paper to get attention by suggesting that you have some benefits to offer or to confirm a verbal presentation. You can't always avoid a written presentation, of course, but don't choose that vehicle over a personal presentation. It's too easy for the decision-maker to say no to paper.

6. Prepare a fallback position

Big ideas run into big objections which are often impossible to overcome. If practical, have ready a minimum-risk version of the proposal. Or work out a piecemeal version that top management may be willing to try on a let's-see-what-happens basis. Prepare a list of all the possible objections you may encounter and the various ways you can overcome them.

I once watched a manager present a three-part program to her company's executive committee. When she ran into resistance on one of the three parts, she retreated slightly and showed how, by modifying the remaining two components, many of the objectives could be still achieved. She won the approval of the committee for most of the program.

When you are selling yourself or an idea you've developed, an all-or-nothing posture can be disastrous for the ego. Better to come out with something by having workable compromises in mind.

Giving a strong presentation

When you are giving a presentation, one to one, as Bill did over lunch, you have to walk the line between cheating yourself by not getting enough information across and boring the other with a stilted delivery. You want to take advantage of the informality of the setting while making sure that the other one has all the data necessary to make a decision.

Here are some pointers on adding enough "sell" to your informal presentation. When making your presentation, be sure you provide the following:

1. An attention-getting opening statement

Your opening statement must address itself to the here and now. You want to hook your prospect's attention with:

- A statement that has currency: "The energy crunch is affecting our department in more ways than one."
- A statement that is factual or that can easily be proven: "Productivity in that department has been flat as a pancake for the past five years."
- A statement that cannot be disputed or with which the prospect is likely to agree: "Keeping costs down in this time of inflation is a real priority for us."

Prospects will identify with statements that reflect the constraints under which they are working. They are sensible, pertinent, and safe statements that will get a nod, not a nay. You begin by talking current sense, so the prospect listens.

2. A benefit statement that follows directly from the opening statement

A good benefit statement does these things:

- Picks up directly from the prospect's agreement to the opening: "Chances are we can save 15 to 20 percent."
- Sticks to a single major benefit that is predictable, because it stems

from your opening: "I have a plan that can increase productivity without increasing costs."

- Is based on a premise to which the prospect has already agreed. Prospects are not about to ignore a cost-reducing benefit, for example, if that is what they agreed is important to them in the opening exchange.

3. A *sequence of facts that add up to a story*

The body of the presentation is factual, but does it have a story line? Fact piled upon fact can be either impressive or boring. The body of fact needs to be presented with a clear story line, so that it is interesting, makes sense, and builds.

A good sequence of facts is orderly and logical, allows for easy retention of key points, and keeps fat and clutter to a bare minimum. One way to align your facts is along the sequence of a newspaper story; that is, begin with the most important facts and end with the least. Another alternative is to save something big for last, for a strong close.

4. *Gaps for questions*

Gaps for questions invite the other person to get into the act without being asked. A question gap is created by leaving out of the presentation certain facts you want the prospect to inquire about and show interest in: "Those, for example, are just two of the steps we can take. There are more, of course." You hope that your listener will ask you to describe one or two of the others.

5. *Gaps for closes*

Gaps for closes make it easy for you to try for the order rather than finish out the presentation. There is something wrong with your presentation if you must deliver it to the last line before asking for the order. Gaps should be built in throughout to enable you to at least test the listener's interest in what you are saying. For example, suppose a prospect responds to the question gap about the various steps. You respond by describing the other options, and then ask which of the options makes most sense.

A good reason for structuring the presentation of facts along newspaper-story lines is that no matter when you attempt a trial close, your listener already has the most important facts. They are often all he or she needs to make a decision.

It takes a lot of skill to make an informal presentation. You want to keep it loose enough so as to encourage a dialogue, but you have to maintain control so that you don't get too far away from your objective. Furthermore, you don't want to prattle on forever. You have to be vigilant and yet look fairly relaxed and confident. And, of course, you have to preserve a sufficient emotional detachment that you don't become defensive. (There's more about defensiveness later in the chapter.)

Pushing the campaign

Have you ever watched in dismay as a proposal of yours, as it goes up the line or through a committee, gets "improved" to make it more salable or more practical? You propose, but others dispose. And it hurts to see your "baby" transformed and remolded.

It is a fact of organizational life that ideas belong to no one person. Yet many managers who originate a plan, design, or project feel impelled to fight for what they consider the integrity of the idea. Often, though, the originator has an exaggerated concept of the idea's worth—or of the threat to its integrity. Taking up the cudgels may do extensive damage both to the person and to the proposal. So, if you're tempted to go out on a limb, ask yourself these two questions:

1. Are you fighting for the idea or for your pride?

Trying to stay detached is nearly impossible. But you can recognize the signs that you are too personally involved in what you're doing. For example, when you hear that changes are being made, do you formulate your argument against the revisions before you ask some-one to explain them? Do you feel your idea is being destroyed? Do you complain about the changes to people who are not really in-volved in the action? When colleagues compliment you on the idea, do you tell them you no longer want to be associated with it? You can wind up paying a prohibitive price for pride.

2. Are you prepared to accept the risks of your campaign?

Let's say that you have decided that your primary concern is the project and that its original form must be preserved. You are so convinced of the necessity to protect its integrity that you are willing to risk the displeasure of your colleagues and superiors to fight the thing through. Do you fully appreciate the consequences of your battle if you lose and, just as important, if you win? Will you be able to continue working effectively with your colleagues in either case?

If you decided that some risk is justified, here are some guidelines to help you:

Get some objective advice

You are probably too close to what is going on to think clearly about tactics. Ask for counsel from someone you respect—perhaps a co-worker who is experienced in the organization but not directly in-volved with what you are doing. Don't expect that person to tell you what to do or how to do it. He or she can, however, help you develop a perspective on your strengths and weaknesses. Then you can decide more easily what tactics to pursue.

Take a breather

If possible, get involved temporarily in some other activity. Chances are that this interlude will give you a clearer idea of what is involved. You may even discover that you don't have the strong feelings you thought you had, that you are in fact more flexible and open to accommodation.

Base your campaign on what is actually happening

Be positive. Assume that everyone, ally or not, is operating in the best interests of the organization, as you are. If you attribute unfriendly motives or insincerity to someone, you're likely to make an enemy out of a potential friend.

Figure what you can salvage

Don't get yourself boxed in so that the idea becomes a go/no-go proposition. If your original concept has been substantially altered, you may be able to come up with a second idea embodying some of the aspects of the program that were rejected.

Find the bargaining advantage

It is possible that those who changed your recommendation are conscious that you feel bad about some of the changes. They may sympathize with you, even though they feel that the changes are justified. Perhaps you can use this sympathy to establish a trade-off. They might be willing to give you a favor in return for your support of their alterations.

Put it in writing

When attorneys are unhappy with the ruling a judge hands down in court, they ask that the record show they take exception to the ruling. Why not do this in your case? Let the record show that you disagree. Reading your arguments in a quiet moment may have more effect on those who count than all your previous discussions. A word to the wise: Before sending your comments on, put them away for a day or two. Then take a look at them to make sure you didn't put down anything in the heat of frustration that you would rather not have on record.

Once you have expressed your thoughts in writing, have gotten it into the right hands, and have received *no* for an answer, back off. Go on to something else.

The key to effective action in campaigning for an idea or project is to know when to turn away from it. If you keep pushing despite implacable opposition, you're likely to gain a reputation that will be a handicap the next time you have a proposal to put forward. The decision-makers will be reluctant to entertain your ideas because they don't want the hassle.

Following up

But suppose you don't get a decision—neither yes or no. You may want to get the stalled idea moving again. Persistence in the face of obstacles is a good selling trait. But there is a difference between seeming persistent and coming across as annoyingly obstinate. If you don't come back with fresh reasons for consideration, you may be seen as stubborn and unrealistic.

Here are some steps you can take to come back or follow up:

Present new information

Your new information should tend to disprove the major objection offered by the person you are trying to convince. But you want to avoid making the decision maker feel defensive, so emphasize that it was *your* oversight not to have done all your homework: "I'm sorry I didn't have these diagrams the first time, but, as you can see, they show a way to build a recreation room without disrupting floor traffic."

Ignore the objection completely

Let an interval of time pass. If the objection was presented without much force, you might wait only a few days. If it is presented more vehemently, let a few weeks or more go by. Then you may be able to revive your case by acting as if the objection was never made. Rather than address it, you can simply present a list of new advantages that you had overlooked on the first go-round: "I neglected to point out that training people to do two jobs would reduce our need for temporary help in the summer."

Minimize the objection

If the objection is too important to ignore completely, what are the arguments that might tend to reduce its weight? For example, "I admit that we could postpone resurfacing the area. But if you look at how much costs have been going up, it's safe to assume we'll be paying twelve to fifteen percent more to do the job next year."

Bring along a back-up

When you reopen your case, bring along an informed and friendly witness if you can. "Sally told me about an experience she had that may shed some new light on that security system I had asked you to consider. Could I bring her by tomorrow to fill you in?" When someone is willing to reinforce you with a case history or statistical evidence, you gain a factual as well as a psychological boost for your argument.

Be reassuring about the soundness of the move you're urging

When a higher executive asks for time to think over your proposal and you feel it's a stall that could last indefinitely, you may need to re-emphasize the wisdom of what you're urging. It could be that clearing up an uncertainty will do the trick: "The two companies I know of who've tried the computer say they'd never go back to their manual systems. We could check with them to see why they're so sold."

Although you may prefer to present your new data or arguments in writing, they will be easy to ignore unless at some point you also ask for a face-to-face meeting. And you may still have to ask for the decision in person anyway. So, why not stick your head in the executive's door and say, "You've read my memo? Good—when can we discuss it?"

Controlling your defensiveness

Suppose a colleague walked into your office after the two of you had been in a meeting at which your project was discussed, and, without preamble or warning, said, "You know, I wish you'd thought that through more before you brought it up. It's a good idea but it needed more work." What happens in you? You probably wonder, why is he telling me this? What are his motives? Why is he criticizing me? You become frustrated. You feel a need to defend yourself. Perhaps you become a bit indignant. You sense an attack, and you defend yourself.

Some people are more defensive than others. No doubt you've encountered people who read sinister or pejorative meanings into seemingly innocent statements. But nearly all of us have defensive mechanisms to repel a threat. It isn't a time for thinking; it's a time for doing.

Acting on your instinctive defense reactions is a problem when you want to maintain some kind of control over the situation. Say your boss shows up in the doorway of your office and says, "I want to know why you haven't done what I asked you to do on the Guthrie project." You have good reasons. If you could say to the boss, "Come on in. Sit down. Let me tell you what's happening," everything would be straightened out. But your heart pounds, your face flushes, your voice trembles. The words don't seem to come out right.

You are not effective.

If you can think back and identify moments when you become defensive, you're ahead of many people who don't even like to admit that they react defensively. Think about how you wish you had reacted—calmly, logically, and in control. You can develop these calm and effective ways of dealing with a perceived attack.

Perhaps the simplest way to deal with a threat is to delay the reaction. After all, the other person isn't coming at you with a lance or a sword whose blow must be instantly deflected. The weapon is words. If they're not answered immediately, what's the harm?

One delaying tactic is to say nothing. Time is a resource for you. Start collecting your thoughts. You can gain even more time by signaling the other person that you didn't catch everything the first time around. You looked perplexed, say, "I'm sorry?" That usually forces the other person to repeat.

You can repeat the charge or statement. "Why haven't I done what you asked on the Guthrie project?" Pause. Be thoughtful. However, if you pause too long, you may be met with anger: "Yes, that's exactly what I said. Do you want me to write it for you?"

If you really are in control, you can reply, "Well, I think I can give some pretty good reasons why." Keep your voice level. The lower the register the better. "Sit down, and let's talk about it." Your calm, confident approach may help to diminish the force in the attack and help the other person to be more receptive.

Sometimes acknowledging the other person's feelings can give you more space for yourself. "You seem to be very angry with me." The other person will either admit it and explain why, or will deny it. In the case of admission, you've gained time and information. Denial will usually result in a change of behavior, in other words, a move to lessen the appearance of anger. The other person probably will want to disprove that he or she is angry. Even if the response is, "You're right; I'm angry," your refusal to get rattled will usually blunt the force of the anger.

Control is the key word in nondefensive communication. When you make a defensive reply, you lose control of the situation. You surrender control to the person who has made you feel attacked. Once you lose control, you will probably undermine your effectiveness. You will have committed yourself to a course of action—anger, justification, debate, whatever. To be effective, do not respond before it is necessary or desirable to do so. Training and practice can help overcome what is the function of nature—to defend oneself when attacked.

An important point to understand is that you may not really be under attack. You have to test your perception. Ask yourself, "What is going on here? How can I respond most effectively?" Practice gaining time so that you remain in control.

When you retain control over the situation, you have a better chance of getting what you want. When you refuse to respond in a defensive fashion, you can generate options: you can say this or that, or you can say nothing. All of your options are measured against what you want to accomplish in the transaction, as initially unpleasant as it might seem.

In short, you can train yourself to respond to apparent or presumed "attacks" on you and your ideas in constructive ways:

1. Pause. Don't lose control by replying "in kind," thereby increasing heat and decreasing light.

2. Get information. What is the other person really doing? Check out your perceptions.

3. Decide what you want out of the transaction, and then ask what the other person might want. For example, the other person wants information (or to express doubts or anger), and I want to convince the other that I am doing the right thing.

4. Develop tactics that will lead to your objective.

Being realistic

To borrow from Oscar Wilde, it is important to be earnest when selling yourself and your ideas. But it is perhaps even more important to be realistic. If you are selling yourself, you have to be able to assess the product—your strengths, your limitations and your abilities. Self-assessment is far from easy. Take a leaf from the salesperson's notebook: you cannot sell strongly without acknowledging the weaknesses of what you are selling.

Realism is not based solely on assessment of yourself or your ideas, that is, how inherently worthy you or they are. You must evaluate your product in terms of the needs of other people or your organization. You can never afford to forget that in persuading other people you must deal with their perceptions of their wants, needs, and objectives. Effective persuasion can help to shape those perceptions, true. But the starting point is always with them.

Remaining in control of your campaign to influence others is one of the most difficult aspects of the selling situation. You must guide, maneuver somewhat, but never push. You must have patience, but not too much. You must have a finely tuned sense of timing: when to start, to stop, to continue, to close.

Persuasiveness is a discipline. Like most professional salespeople, you never cease to work at it.

7

Selling Against Opposition

Salespeople expect opposition. They may not always be prepared for it, but they know there will be a certain buyer resistance. They look at it as a natural, predictable part of the sales transaction. Prospects will say "No," or "I'll think about it," or "I'm not sure I see the value in it." There are any number of ways to put off, or turn down, a salesperson.

But if you don't sell for a living, you may not even expect opposition. If an idea is reasonable, if it makes sense to you, you probably anticipate its acceptance. For example, you want to replace an employee who has quit. It's a routine problem. You tell your boss what kind of a replacement you'd like, and you are stunned when the boss said, "We've just been told to do some drastic cost-cutting, and I'm afraid that hiring a new person now would be hard to justify."

Or you are sitting in a meeting and an idea occurs to you, a solution for a problem that the group is discussing. But immediately after you propose it, one of others at the conference table, "Well, that idea sounds pretty good, but we tried something like it three years ago and we had an awful time getting out of the hole."

Sometimes opposition comes in the form of a stall. You think that streamlining some of the procedures in the flow of work between another department and yours will cut the time required to do certain tasks. The manager of the other department hems and haws and then says, "Well, we can't do this now, although it sounds like a good idea. You see, I'm breaking in a new clerk, and this would only confuse her. Why don't we talk about it again in a couple of months?"

That's a stall, and it is just as effective as a turndown now. You may believe that the issue will be considered again in two months, but the manager may hope it will not come up again.

If you want to be successful at selling your ideas, you, like the salesperson, must be prepared for some opposition in the form of objections and stalls, even when your ideas seem to have a lot of merit. Always remember that you are the seller. Otherwise, you may become the unwitting buyer of the objections and stalls that are symptomatic of resistance to your idea.

Reasons for opposition

Many people get upset when their opinions or proposals are resisted. After all, one's ego and judgment are involved. When people say no to you, when they disagree with you or the value of your ideas, you may feel personally rejected, or at least discounted. Sometimes, of course, the objection may be rooted in personal feelings: the objector doesn't like you, or is envious of you, or is competing with you.

Most salespeople know that most opposition is not personally directed at them. There's an old story about the young salesman who came into his branch office one afternoon obviously in a disturbed and angry state. An old-timer was sitting at a desk nearby and asked what the matter was. The younger salesman described getting turned down on an important sale, and he described the prospect as rude. "I've never been so insulted in my life," he said. "Does this happen very often?" he asked the old man, who shook his head. "Let's see," the old-timer thought aloud, "I remember being punched in the face once, and another time I was pushed down a flight of stairs, and my sample case was thrown down in the street and stomped on, but I can't remember ever being insulted." That's making a fine distinction, one that may elude most of us, but the old pro realized that much opposition is not personal.

There are several points to keep in mind when you are trying to sell something. Many times people have no well-grounded, logical reasons for resisting an idea or a plan. Probably they really haven't thought through the position they are maintaining. (Often their position is borrowed from someone they admire or upon whom they depend.) When you give them a new idea, you force them to really think through the old. And they may resist doing that.

Other reasons people resist being influenced include loyalty toward an old way of doing things or toward someone else who may think differently. (In the life insurance field, the sales rep is always competing against the ubiquitous brother-in-law who's in the business.) Certain people may not trust you at first. They may not believe what you say, or that you are capable of doing what you say you can do.

Simple inertia is among the principal reasons why people resist your efforts to introduce change. You want to persuade me to do something that I'm not doing now, or to stop doing something that I am doing. It seems easier for me to continue the way I am.

Others are not so much for one position as resistant to the notion of changing. They're automatically afraid that a change will bring some disadvantage to them. Incidentally, it's a good thing to remember that most people do not necessarily resist change per se. That's a myth. What they resist is what they think is being done to them through the change. What you must do is show what is being done *for* them in the change.

The logical facade

Resistance, no matter what its roots, often assumes an outward form that appears logical. Yet the real reasons for the resistance may have little or nothing to do with logic. If you try to meet opposition on a strictly rational basis, you may miss the target entirely. For example, manager Jones has a long-time subordinate, Smith, who has been working in a clerical function for years. Smith tends to be somewhat proprietary about the way he does his work, sticking with methods that he devised years ago. He is conscientious but seemingly suspicious of attempts to persuade him to do things differently.

The manager learns of a seminar that will take several days and will review techniques and work methods that apply to Smith. He tries to interest Smith in attending the seminar at company expense, but Smith holds back. The manager employs a number of persuasive arguments. For instance, Smith has been working very hard, and the seminar will offer him a change. What he learns there will make his job easier and more enjoyable. Furthermore, Jones hints, there might be a promotion in the offing.

He is surprised by Smith's continuing resistance. It is the busy season, Smith argues. Another employee is out sick, and the department cannot afford to fall behind in the work, as it certainly will if Smith leaves for several days. There is also an important job with an imminent deadline. On and on go the reasons why Smith should not go at this time. They are all quite logical. But the truth is that Smith is frightened. He is worried about having to learn new ways of doing his job. He is insecure about his position in the department. What changes will the manager make while he is away, he wonders.

Smith has manufactured logical explanations for his reluctance. He may not even be aware that that is what he is doing.

Change as others see it

Thus when you attempt to forecast the amount of resistance there will be to any given change, you must deal not with what your objective view of the plan is, but with how it may be perceived by the people who will be affected by it. There may be a big difference between the plan and the perception of it. For example, in a reorganization of office space, four secretaries, each of whom formerly sat at a desk outside her respective boss's office, were grouped in one area. The *plan:* The secretaries would now be in a more convenient, more comfortable, better-lit working space, which would enable them to help each other, cover phones, and the like. The *perception:* The secretaries thought of themselves as being downgraded into a typing pool.

In another case, sales call report forms were redesigned to elicit more market intelligence data from the field force. The *plan:* The more detailed form would help the home office computer alert sales representatives to competitive moves that might affect them. The *perception:* The reps felt that they were being saddled with more paperwork, and this would cut down on their selling time.

Employees in one troubled financial operation were informed by management that a consulting firm was being hired to analyze the problems that had plagued employees and management alike. The *plan:* As a result of the analysis and recommendations, employees would experience fewer frustrations and duplications of work loads. Work could proceed more efficiently and easily. The *perception:* Some employees would be judged redundant and would be terminated, and ways would be found for the remaining employees to work much harder than before.

In considering how any change is going to be received, you must place yourself in the position of the people who will be affected. Try, as much as possible, to see it from their point of view.

Eight anxiety factors

A study by The Research Institute of America has identified at least eight anxiety-producing factors which are most likely to increase resistance to change in others. Knowing what they are and anticipating these reactions can go a long way toward helping you allay anxiety in those to whom you propose a new idea. These factors and related questions are:

Threat to security

Will the change appear to cut earning potential? Will it make people seem more replaceable? More vulnerable? Will jobs be terminated?

Diminution of self-esteem

Will the change tend to make people "cogs in the machine?" Might it cut down the areas in which they exercise independence? What self-images will be affected by this change?

Diminution of status

Will some people come out looking less important than before? Whose status is elevated, and whose is reduced? How would people explain this change to family members, friends, and co-workers?

Inconvenience

What established routines will be upset? Will anyone have to spend more time away from home? Get up earlier? Do more paperwork? Plan differently? How well established are the patterns that will now be altered?

Work and pressure

Who will have to work harder? Will those people be subjected to greater pressure? Will the rewards for greater effort or stress be clear to them?

Environment

Are different physical surroundings involved? Will this be clearly seen as an improvement? To what extent have the people involved settled in to the present environment? What will be seen, heard, and felt in the new setup?

Human contact

Will people be exposed to new faces? Will friends see each other less? How will existing relationships among colleagues or with customers be affected? How many people will have different bosses? How will they react to them?

Past experience

What changes have people been subjected to before? What were their reactions? Did results match promises? Have they talked negatively about other changes?

All these are "seed" questions, designed to start your mental processes flowing. As you consider those affected by an impending change, you will undoubtedly think of many more.

Granted, opposition to your ideas or plans can be distressing. But take comfort if the opposition is overt rather than covert. Remember the admonition "Work for a 'no.'" Sell for a yes, of course, but barring a positive answer, try hard to get specific opposition—an outright turndown, hesitation, an objection or a stall. Then you can try to uncover the reasons why opposition is being expressed. At least you know it's there, and you are not surrounded by smiles of people who assure you that all is well for you when in fact it is not.

Force field analysis

Experienced persuaders understand that when you exert force (persuasive force), a counterforce develops. Kurt Lewin, the eminent psychologist, pointed out years ago that, if you wish to effect change, you must increase the force while you decrease the counterforce. His technique for studying this phenomenon is called Force Field Analysis, and it is useful for anticipating the kinds of resistance you might receive when you attempt to influence others.

Force Field Analysis may be a more elaborate technique to anticipating opposition than you have been accustomed to using. After all, in many cases you can simply draw up a list of pros and cons. And by the way, when you are dealing with resistance, sometimes that's a good way of drawing out what is really bothering the other person. Say something like, "Well, let's think up as many points in favor of and against that we can." Draw a line down the middle of the paper, label one side "pro" and the other side "con" and begin. Such a simple list has some drawbacks, though. For example, some pros are stronger than others, and so are some cons. An analysis of the force field enables you to visualize dynamics that a simple list may not show.

Force Field Analysis is a systematic approach to thinking about what is involved in making a change. It can help you identify the forces pushing for change, those resisting it, and those that might be intensified or reduced in order to allow the change to be made.

The diagram below illustrates any situation before change. The centerline is the current state of equilibrium, in which driving forces are neutralized by restraining forces.

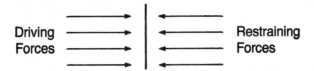

Driving Forces   Restraining Forces

Below are listed some of the driving forces that, from one company's point of view, would justify the reorganization of sales territories. They are factors that management thinks will make the potential in the new territories more equitable and profitable for both salespeople and the company. The heavier lines indicate those forces that are felt to be stronger or take higher priority. They are the forces that demand special attention.

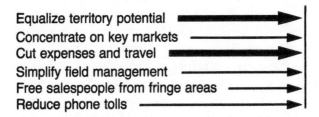

Equalize territory potential
Concentrate on key markets
Cut expenses and travel
Simplify field management
Free salespeople from fringe areas
Reduce phone tolls

Now here is a list of the restraining forces, those that may lead sales reps to resist the change in territory structure.

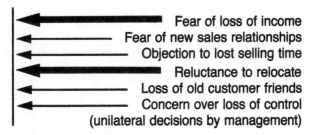

Fear of loss of income
Fear of new sales relationships
Objection to lost selling time
Reluctance to relocate
Loss of old customer friends
Concern over loss of control
(unilateral decisions by management)

By using Force Field Analysis, you can identify those driving forces that offer chief benefits and the restraining forces that likely represent the most resistance. The way to move beyond the center-line status quo to the desired change is to weaken the restraints imposed by the sales force and strengthen the drives as part of a single campaign. Therefore, two sets of forces are analyzed separately, but dealt with together.

Some of the resistance to relocation, for example, *can* be overcome by fiat: relocate or leave. The newness of the sales relationships can be eased by having new sales reps introduced by those moving on. And the fear of lost income can be handled by crediting reps with business from former accounts during a transition, settling-in period. Some of the concern for loss of control might be eased by bringing the salespeople, or a representative task force, into the decision-making process, so that the people in the field would have some say.

To create the impetus that the driving forces will bring, the sales force gets a positively oriented explanation: As profits are increased and costs cut, the financial security of each salesperson in the territory will be enhanced. Reduced travel time will mean more time with their families. And easing field managers' burdens will allow more time with each sales rep—usually a plus for everyone involved.

In addition, a new compensation plan may be introduced to reward sales reps for opening accounts in territories new to them. That will tend to add power to the drives, by making the new territory look inviting.

You can use Force Field Analysis to help anticipate the benefits of your idea or plan and the resistance that others might express to it. By analyzing, you can see the points at which you can be most persuasive, and you can pinpoint the counterforces that can be weakened. It's a valuable tool for preparing a presentation. Try it the next time you are planning to persuade your boss to give you a raise, expand your responsibility, or when you'd like to influence a fellow manager to adopt a more cooperative plan. It can be useful in finding ways to convince subordinates of doing tasks in a different way. It's even useful for developing reasons your family should settle on two weeks at the lake instead of a trip to Disneyland.

In each case, list for yourself the driving forces on your side and the restraining forces for the others. Then try to redefine the driving forces as benefits for the others. You might be able to show, for example, how your plan for greater cooperation with another manager might ease his or her burden as well as yours. Or that the result of your new efforts in tandem could produce results that would bring credit and visibility to you both. (Force Field Analysis is primarily a planning tool for you. It may be cumbersome to use as a visual aid during a presentation.)

One pitfall of preparing for objections

No salesperson would think of making a sales call on a prospect without trying to anticipate the objections that might be raised to buying whatever is being offered. It would be just as shortsighted for you not to expect opposition to some of your ideas and suggestions. However, successful persuaders are careful not to become preoccupied with speculation on possible objections. Otherwise they might load their presentations with points that head off the objections but make their arguments sound defensive. And often it is a defensive presentation that actually puts the objection in the listener's mind in the first place.

For example, a salesman who expects a price objection ("It costs too much" or "Your price is out of line") usually will take steps to head it off. But that could be a mistake. During the presentation he might refer to the "reasonable," "highly competitive," or "surprisingly inexpensive" price. If the prospect is indeed worried about cost, these references might help allay those fears. But if cost is not one of his special concerns, frequent references to price may cause him to wonder why the salesman is dwelling on it—and then suspect that the salesman is defensive about the price with good reason. The salesman, by anticipating the objection, has created it.

Similarly, you may be presenting a plan to a committee made up of several of your peers from finance, manufacturing, purchasing, etc. A co-worker has suggested that the production manager might have some objections to your ideas for revamping the materials management system. You take precautions by inserting as many assurances into your presentation as you can that whatever problems are created by the changes will be offset by other benefits. The production manager may not have been concerned—that is, before you talked so much about it. You have helped raise a question in his mind, though, and hence some opposition that you might have avoided.

Good sales advice is, know what kind of armament you may face—but don't assume that it will all necessarily be trained on you.

Be slow to respond

When you meet opposition, you have a choice of reactions. You can wade right in and answer it. If the opposition is heated, you can generate some heat of your own. You can ignore it. You can rise above it all and refuse to "dignify" it. You can stall.

Many people are tempted to jump right in and answer the objection immediately. Why do they respond so quickly? Well, it seems natural. Someone has a problem accepting the idea, and all that's needed is to clear up the problem pronto. Besides, they don't want the opposition to take root, so the sooner they meet the objection, the less able it is to get established in the mind of the objector. They also want to appear confident. They've thought it through, they know what they're talking about. A fast answer builds credibility, doesn't it? Perhaps. A quick response can also suggest defensiveness, a lack of confidence, or an offensive overbearingness.

Don't be in a rush to meet and demolish the opposition. There are several reasons to hold your peace. Remember Sheila Layton in Chapter 2? She let the buyer's objection go by. One reason, you'll recall, is that there was no definite way to know whether the expressed objection was the true reason the person was resisting. The prospect who protests to the insurance agent that he already has too much life insurance may really be squeamish about having to think of his own death. The salesperson who presents statistics showing that he is in fact woefully underinsured, considering his survivors, wouldn't begin to reach the essence of the problem. The boss who says the climate in the organization is not right for the adoption of your plan may be covering up the fact that she does not fully understand what you are proposing. You often don't know just how real the objection is. But you can almost be sure that if it is real and serious, it will surface again. The objector isn't going to forget it.

Seeming defensive is a bad image to convey, and it could hinder the acceptance of your ideas. Furthermore, by meeting an objection vigorously, you may discourage your opposition from being open and above-board. Once the opposition is suppressed, you are in trouble. The resistance will continue, but you won't always recognize it as such. You may force it underground not only because you are vehement in your response, but because many people find anything that resembles conflict to be embarrassing. They don't like awkward situations; they don't want to hurt you. They fear an argument. They'll still resist you, but more covertly.

No doubt you have had the experience of sitting on a committee listening to an enthusiastic proponent of a solution argue the case for it so vigorously and at such length that other members chafed. Sometimes good ideas are passed over because people resent the ways in which their proponents defend them. The damage can be even more far-reaching. One manager nearly destroyed her ability to influence higher management by her stubbornness and vehemence in arguing against opposition. The president of her company was overheard saying, "We turn her down and she keeps bringing it up again. And each time she does, we'll turn it down." That is an example of opposition that has hardened so much that a manager has lost the power to be persuasive.

If the opposition remains out in the open (where it should be), you may be tempted to debate it. You think, "Well, that's fine, it gets the issues out on the table." That's not necessarily true. The people on the other side may not have thought out their position, even though they've given you the same objection two or three times. Your challenge may lead them to think they have to justify themselves. The debate that follows may not, after all, have much substance or shed much light on the issues. What may happen is polarization of sorts, a hardening of respective positions. You've undoubtedly seen this many times: positions maintained that are based principally upon pride and not on substance. The gap becomes very difficult to close.

If you are in a group, there is additional good reason not to be too hasty in defending your position: others may do it for you. Usually there will be much more weight given to someone else's defense of your position than to your own. Sometimes people who are not especially sympathetic to your ideas become sympathetic toward you if they feel that the opposition is harsh, premature, or disproportionate. That's a good argument for not permitting yourself to become bellicose. You don't want to lose the sympathy vote. Stay cool at least long enough to give others a chance to help you.

Above all, avoid getting into a shouting match. You've seen it happen. People start out talking relatively calmly. The proposal is advanced, the opposition begins to take shape, the proposal's proponent defends, the opposition justifies and fights back. Before long, people on both sides of the fence are literally shouting at one another, attacking both the proposal and one another, and everything bursts into a storm of ill will.

What brought this about? Inadequate information, in most cases. It's true that there might have been some ill will to begin with, on one side or the other or both. But in most cases the ill feelings come not so much from bias as from frustration. The people who are taking strong positions don't really have enough information, probably haven't done enough thinking, to warrant their positions. So instead of defending, explaining, and trying to achieve understanding, they go on the attack. It's a futile, painful, destructive experience for everyone.

Never jump in too quickly to defend your ideas, opinions, or proposals if they are met with opposition. Instead, use basic selling skills to help you be more effective in meeting that opposition and getting the results you want.

How to react to objections

When dealing with opposition, keep in mind that your objective is to win acceptance of your idea, proposal, or request—not to out-talk or score points so you win the debate. Your objective is to bring others around to your way of thinking. Try to avoid making any statements that divert you from this goal. Above all, stay in control. Don't ignore objections or statements of apparent disagreement. Acknowledge them, but don't react or respond too quickly. It may not be easy, especially when someone seems to be attacking your position. Here are several steps you can take when you have to overcome objections:

1. Relax

Sit back in your chair. That's a specific behavior you can rehearse. Cross your legs. That suggests less tension than keeping both feet firmly on the floor. Keep your facial expression attentive but free from frowns. When you look relaxed, you not only appear confident, but you also make it easier for others to discuss your proposition openly in front of you. One trap to avoid is the sour face. I had a vivid demonstration of how disadvantageous this trap can be while sitting in on a task force a few years ago. One man was quite vocal, not at all hesitant to express his opinions. Yet when someone else even demurred slightly with his opinion or that of someone he supported, he would get the most disagreeable expressions on his face that clearly conveyed messages such as, "What nonsense!"

I stopped the proceedings a few times to say to him, "You seem to be having some strong feelings about what is being said here."

His response was a startled "What? I haven't said anything."

"No, you haven't," I acknowledged. "But your face seems to register very strong emotions."

As I grew to know him better, I became quite sure that I was correct: his thoughts were precisely registered on his face. But he didn't realize the impact his facial expressions were having on others, who felt put down. As a result, this manager was often ineffective with his peers. And when, again unconsciously, he did this in meetings with higher management, he created impressions that were very unfavorable to him with people who had power over him. In spite of my feedback, he never did learn to control his facial expressions and he was never effective.

2. Listen

Listening's not easy, either, when you want to talk, especially when you're sure you have the answer to demolish any reservation in the other person's mind. On one occasion, when I was a salesman, I finished my presentation, expecting to close the deal. The prospect said, "Well, it looks like a pretty expensive program." I broke in with a recap of the presentation, which took at least five minutes. He listened patiently and, when I was finished, he said, "As I was saying, this does seem like a lot of money, but it looks as if I can get some good out of it." I got the order, although I almost got in my own way because I wasn't willing to sit back and listen to what the prospect wanted to say.

It is important to listen because when we don't, we commit two sins. First, we don't learn what we could have by paying attention to the other. Second, we needlessly offend the other person who feels that he or she has the right to express an idea or an opinion.

Maintain frequent eye contact while you listen, so the other person knows that you value what is being said. What you're hearing can provide you with the key to persuading the other person. Furthermore, you're also getting some indication of how effective you are in stating your case. You may be getting a second chance.

When you present an idea to a group and meet resistance, it is even more important to appear to relax and to listen carefully. In a group presentation, the sale is more than halfway made when one person in the group begins to tell the others what a beneficial decision this would be.

Another reason to listen carefully in a group is to find out, if you don't already know, where the power is. You may suspect that people will be inclined to line up with John, who has expressed some reservations about your proposal. To your surprise, when Jim gives you mild support, people begin to reinforce what Jim says. Even John admits suddenly that his reservations are mild indeed. The important fact to remember here is, when possible, avoid meeting people head-on. Go in from an angle, use others to help you when possible. Avoid direct confrontations. And a group gives you more chances for indirect, oblique selling than a one-to-one situation.

3. Accept

"Yes, I certainly agree that there might appear to be a problem." Or, "I can understand how you would feel that way." You don't have to buy the substance of the objection. If you are selling a good product, and a prospect tells you that it is not reliable, or if you're selling an idea to someone and he says your idea is unsound, should you agree? Of course not. What you do is to accept that the prospect *may* really feel that way. You don't know for sure that he or she does. But you should grant the prospect this: that the prospect believes he or she feels that way. There's no value in disputing it. Were you to say, "Why on earth would you feel that way?" or "That's ridiculous," or "Come on, now," what would you gain? An argument, probably. An offended prospect, most likely.

None of us like to have our feelings denied or discounted with suggestions that we don't really know how we feel or that we have no right to feel as we do. Therefore, an important factor in persuading others is to recognize and accept their feelings.

A fascinating and important phenomenon often occurs at this point. The prospect feels a need to elaborate on the reason he or she opposes the proposition. With the salesperson supplying an encouraging smile or a nod, and lots of obvious attention, the prospect explains so much that he discovers that his position is not really so strong as was thought. At that point, the salesperson's ideas begin to make much more sense.

4. Move on

When you recognize resistance, instead of commenting on it, go on to another aspect of your proposal: "Incidentally [although it isn't at all incidental], I was talking about these three-part forms to Ken Winter the other day, and he thought that their use would cut processing time down by several hours. And if you multiply that by two hundred requests each month, we might be able to save seven to eight hundred personnel hours in one month alone!"

That's another benefit. It may divert the opposition; it may not. If it does, you're a big step down the road. If it doesn't, then you'll hear the objection again. "That still doesn't answer the problem we'll have at the computer end. Besides, training people to use this form will consume valuable time."

Now you've heard the objection again, and you may choose to go around it. Wait a while to see whether anyone argues in behalf of your proposal, then throw out another benefit: "You remember that one of the complaints we get most often is that it takes too long to acknowledge the requisitions. It's my estimate, from checking with Frank and Bill, that we might be able to cut 20 percent off the response time."

Yet another benefit. You haven't denied the objection. You simply haven't replied to it directly. If it comes up again, be prepared to deal with it. It's probably the real thing.

Each time you hear the objection, face the person who is presenting it. You may nod slightly, if you wish, to show that you've heard. Don't nod too vigorously, or you'll look as if you're agreeing that there are grounds to the objection. Then you may get the question, "Don't you agree that could be a problem?" If you don't really believe it is, you can always respond, "I sense that you think it could. I'd be interested in your thinking." Great. Now the ball is back in the other court. And you have another chance to listen.

Once you believe that the objection is a substantial one, and that the issue could indeed be a problem, don't try to duck it. Say something such as, "Yes, it could be, and I think there's a way to get around it."

5. *Qualify the objection and answer it briefly*

Now you're ready to qualify the objection, to confirm your suspicion that it is genuine. One effective way to qualify an objection is to restate it as you heard it. "If I hear you right, you're worried about our having to hire one or two more people to get this project rolling. I realize that budgets are tight."

The other person responds with, "Yes, that is a worry. I'm not sure we can justify it."

"If you could justify it, or if we could get by without hiring anyone, either way, how would you feel about going ahead with the project?"

"I'd probably be in favor of it."

You've qualified the objection. It's stamped and certified as the real thing. Now you may feel confident to answer it directly.

When you reach this point, don't try to overwhelm the objection with a long, weighty argument. Choose what you believe is an effective answer to the objection, state it succinctly, then test the reaction of the objector: "Doesn't that make sense?" Or, "Don't you agree?" If you get a positive response, however tentative, you can come back with a more elaborate answer. You are more confident that you're on the right track. However, if the response is not reassuring, switch to another argument, then test that one. Don't get locked into a long answer that doesn't meet the objection. And that won't happen if you remember to keep the other person involved.

In summary, when you run into an objection or a stall, don't be disheartened by what seems to be negative reactions. The fact is, when people voice objections or opposing opinions, they are responding. You've succeeded in getting them involved. There is nothing more disheartening than to get no response or one that is so bland and noncommittal as to give you nothing on which to proceed. Opposition expresses a reaction, even some interest, certainly an opportunity for you to continue, and gives you data with which to continue. An objection may also provide you with the chance to ask for action after you've answered it. Or, in sales parlance, to ask for the order.

8

Techniques That Resolve Conflict

Occasionally resistance can deepen, take root and spread, and become out-and-out conflict. People working together stop speaking to one another except when business requires it. Entire departments withhold information and cooperation from others. Sometimes there will be outbursts of anger. In other cases, there is only a sense that people have taken and are maintaining strong, perhaps even obstinate, contrary positions.

A case study

The following case study, sent to The Research Institute of America readers for their analysis and comment, illustrates a somewhat extreme case of how opposition can erupt into conflict.

George Maynard drummed his fingers on the desk as he waited to read the memo he had just dictated to his secretary. It would be a relief, he felt, to bring the matter to a close, as well as to get out from under the intense anger he was feeling. Quietly his secretary entered the office and placed the memo on the desk. It read:

TO: *Harlow Hutchins*
FROM: *George Maynard*
SUBJECT: *Task force on distribution*

This is to advise you formally that I can no longer justify the time, effort and expense of Phil Dugan's participation on the task force which you head to formulate new distribution systems. His withdrawal is effective immediately.

In view of the disappointing progress of the task force, I do not think it is feasible for me to appoint a replacement. I regret having to take this action.

As Maynard signed his name, his secretary asked, "You said you wanted copies to go to all corporate executives?"

He nodded.

"Blind distribution though?"

"No. I might as well be open about it. I want everyone concerned to know what I'm doing—and that includes Harlow."

A few minutes later, after his secretary had returned from personally distributing the memo, Maynard took a deep breath and told her, "I hate like the devil to do it, but it's the only way. I owe it to Phil. He's been complaining for weeks that what little work the group was doing seemed to land in his lap. I owe it to myself, too—having to do without Phil, never able to find him when I needed him because he was doing Harlow's dirty work. Don't you agree?"

"Well—" his secretary said tentatively.

"Look," Maynard continued, "I tried to tell Harlow. At first I kidded him about my having given up my best man. But today I really have had it. I was totally rational when I talked to him. I was determined not to get upset. I said to him, 'Look, Harlow, this is getting a bit much. I haven't been able to get together with Phil for two minutes this week. I've got work piled up that I can't give him.'

"But you know what? Harlow said that Phil exaggerated. Then he asked, didn't I think it was necessary to modernize our distribution? That really bugged me. I mean, that he would have the nerve to suggest I wasn't for efficiency. I told him I just couldn't see letting my operation go to hell for his task force.

"He didn't even shut his office door. His voice got very loud—I guess everybody in his side of the building could hear. He said that if Phil Dugan worked as hard and as often as he griped, the work would get done and everyone would be happy.

"I was so damned mad all I could think of was to get out of there.

*Well, I'm sorry it has to come to this, but if he wants my cooperation
he is going to have to go about it differently."*

Maynard waited for his secretary's comment, but she never got a
chance to speak. There was a brief knock and Adam Poole, the company controller, stuck his head around the door. "Hey, you coming
to lunch with us?"

"Right." He got up and followed Poole out to the elevators, to join
the other two managers already there. Maynard heard the elevator
bell, indicating the car was coming, just about the time he heard
Harlow Hutchins back in his office demanding to know "where the
hell" he was. Two seconds later Harlow was striding towards the
group by the elevator. Maynard's memo was in his hand.

"Did you have to do this?" he demanded angrily.

"Yes, I did," Maynard responded.

"To everybody in the whole company? I know damned well you
don't like me, but do you have to bury me in manure?"

"I didn't feel I had a choice."

"You didn't have a choice?" Hutchins moved closer, throwing off
the restraining arm of one of the onlookers. "Get away. I'm going to
hit the sonuvabitch."

Maynard saw the fist coming but not in time to duck. He took it
right on the chin. He felt his knees buckle. Someone grabbed him
before he hit the floor, and from his slumped position he saw the
rapidly disappearing back of Harlow Hutchins.

Readers' analyses

Of the large number of readers who responded to the case, many
understood Harlow Hutchins's anger, even if they weren't sympathetic toward the extreme action that he took. Several felt that
George Maynard really threw the first punch. One explained: "Maynard attacked Hutchins, in writing, with copies to all kinds of corporate executives. He openly accused Hutchins of incompetence."

Another wrote, "While I do not condone Harlow's aggressive action, I feel it is merely the culmination of a series of prior events."

That series provides an excellent example of how, when conflict is mismanaged, it can create far-reaching and long-lasting damage. Here are some of the issues that readers singled out:

First of all, Maynard accepted Phil's complaint that what little work the group was doing seemed to land in his lap. The manager should have investigated the complaint and gathered information first hand.

Secondly, Hutchins was too close-mouthed. One reader pointed out the importance of a task force manager's providing regular factual progress reports to other managers who have contributed people to the group. More open communication from Hutchins would have helped Maynard judge whether the task force was progressing and whether the amount of time Dugan was spending on it was justified.

Third, there was no negotiation. Neither manager seemed to recognize the need to negotiate time and priority. More specifically, how much time should the borrowed employee expect to be away from his normal assignments, and under what circumstances does each job, the permanent or temporary one, take priority?

Lastly, Maynard's kidding was a tactical error. Instead of approaching Hutchins in an open, direct, and serious manner about his concern over Dugan's time on the task force, he joked about what was really a serious matter. Humor, so-called, is a poor substitute for honest confrontation of issues.

Thus a history of poor communication, concealment of opinions and genuine feelings, acceptance of second-hand information with all of its bias, a lack of involvement of others, and an absence of concern for their needs, culminated in a serious public put-down and physical attack. The series of steps could have been interrupted, and the ultimate consequences avoided, at any time.

Interestingly, few respondents felt that Hutchins should have been fired for the attack on Maynard. Most agreed that if Hutchins was considered a good man for the organization, if this was an isolated incident, and if either man was under unusual pressure, firing was not the answer. Furthermore, as one reader noted, "If I were higher management, I would think that this action was a direct reflection as to how the organization was being managed."

Conflict—constructive or destructive

Few people are comfortable with conflict. They're anxious, embarrassed, under stress. But a certain amount of conflict can be an indicator of health because it means things are getting done. Ideas and plans are being proposed, opposed, and considered. Campaigns are being launched to get them accepted. Where conflict does not seem to exist, usually nothing is happening or the conflict is being suppressed. In the latter case, conflict is present, under the surface. Unfortunately, just because conflict is pushed under, and held there, doesn't mean it isn't doing its dirty work. People take elaborate measures to keep it hidden, and the energy they expend to keep it from surfacing could be put to constructive purposes. There will be innumerable slights, refusals to cooperate, procrastination, gossiping, all indicating that a deeper problem exists. However, the conflict never surfaces so that people can deal with it.

Thus, conflict can be constructive if it motivates people to get things done. But more often than not, it is destructive in three major ways:

1. It gets personal

Probably the dispute started over an issue or an idea that wasn't sufficiently resolved. If it continues, people shift their attention away from the issue that divided them and direct it to a personal level involving the combatants. Soon the arguments take the form of attack on people rather than on the issues. To illustrate, in our earlier scenario, Hutchins tried to undermine Maynard by suggesting that he wasn't in favor of modernization of the distribution systems. That was a cheap shot.

2. It leads to polarization

A fight that has gone on too long or become too fierce results in a polarization of people and issues. People get locked in and don't know how to get out. They've spent so much time and energy explaining and defending their respective positions that they can't seem to move away from them. There is also pressure to save face. What usually happens is that each side demands that the other make the first concession. You see this often in labor-management strife, when a strike goes on for weeks and labor and management negotiators no longer take the trouble to sit down together. The two sides are frozen in opposition. In the case of Maynard and Hutchins, you can see how Maynard began to do his screaming publicly but at a distance. In many organizations you can hear lots of screaming across chasms.

3. The main issues are lost

Once in a while a conflict goes on so long that no one is certain what started it. The original issue is no longer important. New issues are invented and old ones are re-invented to keep the fire smoldering. It's very discouraging for those on either side who prefer to be noncombatants. The tradition works against them. Incidentally, it really wasn't up to Maynard to judge the effectiveness of the task force. He dragged the issue in to justify his decision to pull Phil out.

When issues give way to personalities, when parties are polarized, when problems become fuzzy, the conflict has become unhealthy.

How to handle a flare-up

In almost every organization or group there are people who try to defuse conflict by shutting it off. These people are especially active in meetings, resorting to such devices as, "I think we're off the subject" or "Let's not get emotional." These are two common shut-off techniques. Under these circumstances, conflict over an issue, however justified and real, receives a stamp of disapproval. Since the conflict is not rational, it is therefore not acceptable. Thus, it is not worked through and resolved. It goes underground to do its harm covertly.

The only real hero in an organizational conflict is one who takes steps to bring the conflict out in order to deal with it. It's a risky role. But the person who knows how to say, "That is a problem.

How can we solve it and continue to work together?" is of much more value to a group or an organization than the person who denies that the problem exists.

There are several points to keep in mind when a conflict arises:

1. The person on the other side of the conflict has a point of view that is just as legitimate and reasonable to him or her as yours is to you.

2. Consider that the other person may also be uncomfortable about the conflict.

3. The other person is usually willing to accept a solution if you can make it sufficiently attractive. At least he or she can be persuaded to work with you to formulate a resolution of the conflict.

4. It is safer and wiser to keep to the issues in any discussion and avoid any personal arguments.

5. The future is often a more constructive base for discussion than the past. Rather than dwell on what caused the problem and who was at fault, place more emphasis on what can be done to provide a solution or an alternative to the situation that exists now.

The above are rational considerations, and they are good ground rules for confronting conflict. But when conflict comes up suddenly, when it is unexpected, even the most skillful and experienced managers can forget to be rational. When a colleague is angry over a missed deadline, or a shipment comes in at a price that is higher than the vendor quoted, or an insurance claim has been denied, there's often a lot of heat and too little light. When your word or pride or reputation seems to be on the line, anger can take over, dictating your reactions and usually stimulating anger in others.

Surprise can be one's worst enemy. For any kind of confrontation, but especially one that is sudden, the best advice is a fundamental sales principle: Remember your objective. What do you want to accomplish most? A sharp reply may be funny, deadly, or clever, but it may not advance your cause. Who wants to wind up like Maynard and Hutchins?

Suppose, for example, you've just returned from a meeting at which a colleague's proposal was discussed thoroughly and tabled for another meeting. You're not enthusiastic about his proposals, but you're not against them, either. You feel that they merit examination. That's the position you saw yourself taking. You are in favor of the tabling and the follow-up session.

Scarcely have you sat down at your desk before the colleague whose proposal was discussed enters your office, closes the door, and says in an obviously strained voice, "What do you have against me? You sat in there doing everything you could to shoot my idea down. After all the work I've done, I think what you did was unfair. And it isn't the first time you've done this to me." He stands there, jaw tight, an angry look in his eyes.

You have a conflict on your hands, and you not only did not plan it but you feel you didn't do anything to bring it on. What are your reactions? Anger? ("You have no right to come barging into my office saying these things about me. Would you please leave?") Innocence? ("You have it all wrong. I don't want to shoot you down.") Punishment? ("If you are going to behave like a hysterical child, I think you'd better take a walk or splash some cold water on your face and calm down. I don't think you want our colleagues to know about such immature behavior.")

If your objective is to exacerbate your colleague's bad feelings, to escalate the conflict, any of the above responses will do just that. Remember that the other person's opinions and feelings are just as reasonable to him or her as yours are to you (our earlier "point 1"). All three reactions say, "You have no right to be angry." He believes that he does. Impasse.

Realize that the other person may also be uncomfortable about the conflict (point 2). It took a lot of anger for him to come into your office and accuse you. No one is at ease with that much emotion. He wants a satisfactory resolution—a way out—too.

How do you feel? Probably angry, offended, possibly a bit frightened. But what do you want to accomplish? Ultimately, of course, you want to convince your colleague that he is wrong. You want him to accept your view. However, selling is done in stages. Your first order is to calm him down and stop any further verbal assault.

You do this with a response such as, "I'm sorry you feel that way, Mike. It wasn't my intention to shoot you down."

"That's the way it looked," Mike replies.

"I understand that's the way it looked to you. Sit down for a moment, and let's talk about it."

Why should Mike sit down? Because of point 3. He will buy if you give him the benefits. "Look, Mike you're upset, and I don't want you to be. I don't want to be upset myself. Furthermore, your idea is going to come up again next week, and I want to give it a fair shake. Let's talk about it now, if you like."

Mike sits down. Give him a chance to talk. For example, you might say, "What did you see me doing that made you think I was trying to shoot your idea down?"

Try to relax. Listen. Don't jump in to answer or to deny. Let him talk. Insist that he stay on the issues. If he should say, "I thought you were ticked off at me because last month I . . . ," say, "Look, Mike, I'm more interested in what you saw me do today that upset you."

After Mike has talked, follow the rest of the prescriptions (points 4 and 5). "Okay, I still have some unanswered questions about your proposal, and from the discussion, I know that others do also. Would you like me to list them?"

Mike agrees. You do. Then you wind up with, "I'm sorry, Mike, that you saw me as trying to destroy your idea. I wasn't. I'm not against it, but I'm not yet entirely sold on it either. Now how can you help us get the answers to these questions, because they're going to come up again."

You've focused on the future. You've asked for answers. You've proposed an alternative to the situation that exists now.

If you're the one who's angry

Let's assume you were in Mike's shoes—you are angry with someone else and want to express it. You have realized that there is just no point in concealing or suppressing the fact that you're aggrieved. If you're really upset, there's little point in suggesting that you prepare a sales presentation. It would be ideal if you could, but in anger, your presentation would probably be lopsided all in your favor. Even so, there are certain rules that, if followed, will enable you to be more effective than if you just let go.

1. Give fair warning of what you feel

One of the biggest problem-causers in dealing with other people is expressing anger when the other person has no idea it is coming. Probably you have had the experience of offering what you considered constructive criticism, only to have the other person blow up in your face. At the very least, the unexpected anger makes you want to avoid any contact with that person. At most, you get angry, too.

If you feel angry and want to express it, give fair warning of the way you feel. A simple phrase like, "This is starting to irritate me," or "I'm feeling very angry," can be very helpful. What isn't helpful is maintaining a facade of rationality or cordiality while your voice, your gestures, or other physical signs give away your real feelings. Although the other person may not enjoy being confronted with your anger, your direct expression of it is at least a clear, unambiguous message that can be dealt with.

2. Be specific

No matter how a dispute starts, it is likely to be painful. But it can also be profitable if both you and the other person find out what's really bothering each other. State immediately, in as few words as possible, just what it is that's making you hot under the collar. Repeat the cause of your anger frequently, with simple variations in the wording, until you're absolutely certain that you're being understood by the other person. Do not use the occasion to drag in a list of past, unresolved irritants. You want the other person to change the behavior that is annoying you now. It is doubtful that the other person will be willing or able to change if he or she is buried under an avalanche of grievances.

3. Listen

If the other person gets angry in turn, try to make an extra effort to listen. Like you, he may be too excited to be as articulate as he should, and it's up to you to sort out the causes of his anger.

4. Try not to judge motivation

It is enough to say that what the other person has said or done has angered you. He or she can't deny your feelings. If you say something like "You've been looking for a chance to trip me up for weeks," the other person may deny the accusation, and the two of you might never reach an understanding.

A useful opening

If you are the one who is angry, here is a basic opening for handling the confrontation successfully:

"I sense that we disagree, and consequently we're not working together the way we'd like. If I'm right, I'd guess that you're as uncomfortable about this problem as I am. I'd like to work with you to find an alternative to what exists now."

You are not placing any blame as you would be if you were to say, "You're causing me a problem" or "You and I have a problem." You might just receive the response that it's *you* who has the problem. Where do you go from there? It's difficult. Avoid any suggestion of blame. Don't make charges. Suggest that something might be true and check it out.

Your opening doesn't imply a fact. Instead, it uses the words "I sense." Remember that you are the expert in your own perceptions. The other person can dispute the facts of the situation, but not the legitimacy of your feelings and perceptions. Furthermore, using this opening, you are tentatively putting your perceptions on the line. Your willingness to be seen as fallible is usually disarming. Few people will fail to respond to what is a healthy bit of humility on your part. Finally, you don't point the finger of blame. You're not looking for a donkey to pin the tail on. You are saying, in effect,

"If you agree that there is a better alternative to the present situation, would you be willing to work with me to find it?"

People of good will will find it very difficult not to respond positively to that invitation.

Preparing for confrontation

The positive response you hope for from your adversary may not be readily forthcoming. If you anticipate any sort of confrontation, you may need to do a little homework before you initiate any discussion. Sit down ahead of your meeting and draw up four lists. The first has to do with your perceptions of the conflict. What are the problems between you as you see them? For example, Mark's Manufacturing Services department seems to fill my requisitions after those of other groups, even though I think mine have been submitted before theirs.

The second list contains what you believe are the other person's perceptions of the problem. Mark probably believes that I am a bit of a pain, that my complaints are rooted in conceit.

List number three is even more speculative: What kinds of responses do you believe the other person will make to your analysis of the situation? Mark may say that I am mistaken, that he handles requisitions chronologically. On the other hand, he may say he fills requisitions according to what he considers priority of needs. He may also suspect that I delay submitting requisitions, and thus get caught in a crunch of my own making.

The fourth list contains your responses to the other person's perceptions. My response: Mark doesn't seem to recognize that some of my requisitions need prompter attention, that I currently experience delays that are inconvenient and costly.

Now you have some idea as to what might be said during your meeting. You'll be able to look forward to talking and hearing about each other's perceptions and judgments, the pluses and minuses of the respective operations, the deficiencies and the failures.

Remember, though, that the lists are largely speculative, even your part of it, because you cannot entirely trust your perceptions of yourself or your speculations as to the other's perceptions. The lists are to help you define your needs and to anticipate the needs of the other person and the resistance you might encounter. More important, the lists should encourage you to take a closer look at how you may have contributed to the conflict. For example, you may not have made your needs clear to Mark.

At any rate, preparing the lists will help remove some of the element of surprise from the meeting. Above all, they may point you in the direction of a solution: How can I enlist Mark's help when I need certain requisitions filled on short notice? What can I contribute to the solution?

Finding a common solution

Usually, each person or group involved in an argument spends valuable time pointing out what went wrong and who was to blame. Once the cause and the culprit have been identified, progress, if there was any, stops. The problem remains.

Here is a technique to get some real movement started, and to keep it going until the problem is resolved. The idea is to get adversaries to agree on some common objectives and how they can realize them.

Get the data

You might suggest that each of you sit down in a quiet place and answer two questions: What should the other person be doing to improve cooperation between us? What should *I* be doing? Once you have the answers, you can make up four lists:

1. I believe that he should . . .
2. He believes that I should . . .
3. I believe that I should . . .
4. He believes that he should . . .

Edit out complaints and finger-pointing so that you have only positive statements. "He should stop doing such-and-so" becomes "He should start doing such-and-so."

Let's assume you have a problem similar to that which George Maynard and Harlow Hutchins faced in the example that opened this chapter. If you were Maynard, one of your "shoulds" might be: Harlow will estimate each week how many hours he will need Phil Dugan to work on the task force project. If you were Harlow Hutchins, a "should" might be: George will consult me in advance when Phil Dugan is not available for task force assignments.

Define common goals

Now boil down the four lists into one, namely the objectives both of you can agree on.

Specify actions, and responsibilities. At this stage, you need to get action. There are three requirements for your plan to succeed:

- An *outline* specifying what has to be done, step by step.
- A *schedule* showing when each step should be accomplished.
- A *list* designating who will be responsible for seeing that each step is done.

When problems between people arise, managers often spend time looking for ways to restore the status quo. This is often a mistake, because problems provide opportunities to move beyond where you were. A dispute gives the people involved a chance to find new ways of talking about and doing things. In the above technique for finding a solution to a problem situation, you establish the need or the benefit of a solution. Then you work together to see what kind of a solution is best. Then you close—you get action.

When you witness anger

Sometimes you can turn a potential disaster into a leadership opportunity for yourself. Pretend you're in the group when the following exchange occurs:

STEVE: (*to the group*) I really don't see why we should spend valuable time going over John's proposal.

JOHN: Why?

STEVE: Because we've been over it before on other occasions, or something very much like it, and we decided then that it wasn't feasible under the conditions, and those conditions haven't changed. So why waste our time?

JOHN: So you're setting yourself up as the judge of what is wasting time. And you've decided, I guess, that what I've put a lot of effort and thought into is just a waste of time.

STEVE: Now, John, I can see that you've done a lot of work here, but . . .

JOHN: Don't come on now with the conciliation bit, "There, there." I'm not a little kid. You think you speak for the whole group, and frankly I resent it. Stop being so arrogant and let others have a say.

If you were sitting in the group, what would your reaction be? Granted, you may have partisan feelings. Perhaps you believe that Steve does pompously set himself up as group spokesman, and you join with John in indignation. On the other hand, you may share Steve's opinion that John is wasting the group's time with one idea that he continues to re-work.

Regardless of your feelings, you should recognize that this is a potentially damaging situation for the group as a whole. It's not just an embarrassment. If the dialogue continues, it will become impossible for John's proposal to be considered with any shred of objectivity because the discussion will have gotten so overheated. It may also become impossible for anything else to get proper consideration. For one thing, any momentum the group has built up will be slowed or destroyed. (At this point people often seek reasons to adjourn.) If the meeting continues, people who support or feel sorry for John will distrust Steve and will tend to discount his contributions on other issues. They might even give more weight to John's statements on other matters because they want him to feel better. John, out of pique, might limit his contribution or withdraw altogether. In that case, a possible resource for the group has been undercut.

For any group to be effective and use its resources as fully as possible, any of the above consequences spell disaster. Obviously some help should be on the way. This is not a job for a peacemaker ("Come on, fellows, wipe the blood off and shake hands"). It is a job for a sensitive, tactful negotiator. Otherwise these two may paint the entire group into a corner.

So you want to intervene. Your first step is twofold: stop the scrapping and remind the others in the meeting that they have a responsibility in this, too. You might therefore break in with this kind of statement: "Wait a minute. You two have spoken your minds. What about the rest of us? We have a stake in this, too."

You may have to be firm, especially if the two have become a world unto themselves. I've seen people intervene successfully by expressing their anger over the unpleasant and wasteful turn of events. Use soft or hard words as required. Once the action is stopped, move fast. Chances are good that these people are still in the grip of strong emotion. They may feel somewhat sheepish. Rescue them—and the meeting. "John has submitted a proposal to us. In my view, he has a right to ask us to consider it. Steve has expressed his opinion, and he has a right to it. But I'd like a chance to hear what others in the group think about it." You've legitimatized both sides.

This is a critical point. Either Steve or John may start the wrangling again. Don't permit it. Say, "Hey, you both have had your say for now. Give the rest of us a chance." Be prepared to have someone say to you, "What do you think about it?" Don't forget what "it" is. What you've done is suggest that the group consider discussing John's proposal. You don't have to take a stand on the proposal itself before you're ready. Your response can be: "My suggestion is that we discuss John's proposal. What do the rest of you think?"

This kind of question can serve to divert the attention of the group away from Steve, John, and you. It usually takes it away from Steve and John, but maybe not from you. You might be pressed: "What is your opinion of John's proposal?" Your answer: "I haven't made up my mind, pro or con. That's why I want to discuss it."

Don't permit yourself to be pinned down before you want or have to be. Of course, if you have clearly made up your mind, it would be dishonest to say otherwise. State some of your views (you don't have to open up on everything). Or take this approach: "I have a problem with John's estimate of the schedule. I think it would take considerably longer, possibly several months longer. And I wondered how other people felt about it."

By this time you've usually sold your order. You've stopped the argument, encouraged the cooperation of others, and gotten the meeting back on a constructive course.

Everyone can win

When you are engaged in conflict or are the unexpected victim of attack, you do not have to deny or repress your human feelings, but you should aim to retain control of the situation. Keep in mind that you do not need to respond immediately. But listen. Keep your eye on your attacker or critic. Do whatever you can to keep the other person talking. Accept the other person's anger or strong feelings, and realize that the other person feels justified in feeling that way. Realize, too, that your opponent might be ill-at-ease with the situation, and take advantage of the discomfort. Take obvious steps to reduce it. "I'm sure that you dislike this situation as much as I do." When you are able to accept the other person's feelings, you are a long way toward repairing the damage and closing the gap between you.

In conflict situations, you can gain the advantage by being straightforward and responsive rather than covert and devious. Involve the other person in finding a solution. Keep everything open and above-board. If you can initiate the search for solutions, instead of assigning blame, you are well on your way to finding those solutions. You are on your way to making a sale. And everyone wins.

9

Selling Bad News

There is perhaps no greater test of persuasive skills than when something unpleasant must be sold. The salesperson has to advise the customer about an unexpected price increase, or that a shortage of raw materials makes it impossible to supply the quantities requested. The manager has to advise his subordinates that annual compensation increases are being cut back—or one subordinate that he is not qualified for the job he wants.

Who likes to deliver bad news? No manager feels good about denying a raise or a promotion, for example. No one takes pleasure in announcing changes that affect people adversely. Many managers even have difficulty criticizing others for substandard performance.

At the heart of the problem is most people's desire to be liked. They dislike being disliked. Giving unpleasant news, they believe, is one way to become disliked. As a result, people often go to great lengths to soften the blow of the bad news to spare the people who must receive it and to spare themselves, too.

For example, here's a sales manager telephoning one of his men in the field:

MANAGER: Art, I wanted to call you to congratulate you on the Cahn order. I know how long you've been trying to crack that account. It must make you feel awfully good to know that your persistence paid off.

ART: It really does. And this is only the beginning.

MANAGER: Knowing you, I'm sure it is. There ought to be a lot of potential in that company. Anything I can do to help?

ART: Nope, but thanks.

MANAGER: Well, keep it in mind. I want to give you all the help I can. You know, Art, I'm convinced that you could make the top five this year if you want to. You've been slipping a bit in the number of new business calls you make each week. I'll bet if you increased the number of those calls by three or four every week, you'd go right to the top. You're doing a good job, but you could do great.

The fact is that this manager has been wanting to tell Art for some time that the number of new business calls he makes could be increased, but he has been putting it off. Art's success with the Cahn order seems like an ideal opening. Give the bad with the good. It makes the bitter more palatable.

Students of management will recognize this technique as the sandwich method of giving criticism—a hunk of criticism between two slices of praise. It makes criticism more palatable but it is a poor feedback technique. The criticism is diluted by praise, and the praise is contaminated by the criticism.

William Tecumseh Sherman said, "War is cruelty, and you cannot refine it." Bad news is bad news, and you can't make it good. By using the proper techniques, you can make it acceptable. By using poor ones, you make it unnecessarily cruel.

Take what is probably the worst news on the job—firing. It ranks as one of the most traumatic, threatening situations that people can go through. No small wonder that many managers will go to great lengths to reduce the pain. Ironically, in doing so they often do greater damage, inflicting cruelty as well as pain. Here are some of the techniques I have heard managers use in firing subordinates:

The no-fault approach

This is exemplified in the frequently heard statement, "It's just not working out." In some cases, if the job is being phased out or the company is reversing a bad decision, this may be literally true. Unfortunately, it is often just a smokescreen. The firer is trying to protect himself. He does *not* say, "*You* are not working out" or "*I* made a mistake." Thus, there can be no discussion of where the employee, or the boss, failed. All the stunned ex-employee knows is that he is out of luck.

You'll be better off

This approach may reflect the truth—sometimes a job doesn't measure up to a person's talents. But in other cases, the manager who says, "I see you as suited to something more creative than what we had to offer," is trying to avoid criticism—of himself or the other person. Again, the fired subordinate isn't being told anything helpful, since usually he has been willing to do the kind of job for which he was hired. Nothing is said about why he was put in the job to begin with, and why it was never possible for him to do what his employer had in mind, assuming there *was* something specific. And if the employee leaves with the feeling that it really wasn't his fault, when it really was, there is no lesson learned for his next job.

Attrition

Gradually the employee's responsibilities are taken away. The manager may imply that she is being held in reserve for something big, while her former duties are taken over by other employees of less consequence. Or the manager suggests that she spend her time giving thought to the kind of job she'd like to have with the company that really suits her strengths. Then, the boss leaves her on her own. Naturally, few of her colleagues will want to have much to do with her, because she's a loser. This further increases her sense of frustration and defeat. She finally arrives at the hoped-for conclusion—that she'd better find another job.

I cry for you

There are times when a good person has to be fired for no other reason than that the company can no longer afford his or her services, excellent though they have been. In such a situation, some managers tend to sympathize to excess: "Joe, you know how much we've always thought of you here. It's just the damned budget, Joe.

It breaks my heart to bring this up, Joe. I couldn't even sleep last night." On and on until the axe finally descends. At first, Joe may feel sorry for the person who is firing him. Then he feels sorry for himself. Then he feels sore at the world. Finally, he merely wishes his boss would shut up so that he can get out of the office and think about what he is going to do next.

What is wrong with these approaches? They cheat the subordinate by inducing him or her to buy without giving the facts necessary to form a buying decision. What is it that I as a manager want the terminated employee to buy? That I'm a nice fellow? No. I like to be known as a nice person, but that's not the issue. The order that I want from you is your acceptance of the fact that you must begin to pursue your career somewhere else and that you understand the necessity for my decision. That's one of the toughest sales a manager has to make, because it is difficult to be convincing about the benefits of buying one's own termination.

Not only does the terminated employee need to accept the decision, but he needs to know more about what cost him this job. If it was his fault, his insufficiency, he deserves to be told that. It's not fair to let him walk out the door ready to repeat the mistakes that brought about termination.

How to fire someone

Here are some recommendations for giving the terribly sad news of termination to a subordinate:

Get to the point

If you are about to fire a person, there's no point in making small talk. This is an extremely tense moment, and trying to make it casual will increase the tension. Focus on the person, and on the circumstances that have brought about the dismissal. If you do, you'll probably find yourself speaking honestly and helpfully. One technique is to say, "There's no easy way for me to say this. I have to terminate you (or ask for your resignation). I'll talk about it as much as you want. But you should understand that nothing will change the decision. Any conversation will only be to help us both in the future."

It is very important in gaining the other person's acceptance that you make it absolutely clear that the firing decision is irreversible. Otherwise you'll probably find yourself cast in the role of an unwilling prospect while the subordinate tries to sell you on reversing the decision. In this situation it is essential that you never forget that you are the seller.

Be personal

Obviously you deliver bad news face-to-face to the individual affected—never in writing. Do it privately in a business setting, the office. (In the movie "Kramer vs. Kramer," the adman, played by Dustin Hoffman, was taken to lunch by his boss, who then fired him before dessert. Unforgiveable.)

If possible, express your own feelings about what has happened: "I'm sorry for the hardship," or "I wish I didn't have to make this cut," or "I'm proud of the work you've done." Your efforts to personalize the message show that, while the decision may be tough, it's not being executed in cold blood. But express such feelings only if they are genuine. Otherwise, stick to the facts.

Listen to people's feelings

Don't rush to give a speech that justifies your move. That won't make the news easier to take. It could, in fact, make it more infuriating. Your credibility and sincerity are of inestimable value in getting acceptance by the terminated employee. You can't afford to say anything that will undermine those qualities. Describe the facts and your feelings as they are. Don't minimize facts and exaggerate feelings. The terminated employee may not like you or the experience but will have to respect you. Even more important, your honesty in this situation will build even more credibility with employees who are left.

Dealing with feelings

Recently I was invited by a company's management to sit in on a large interdepartmental meeting at which a substantial reorganization was to be announced. Rumors of such a move had been circulating, and the expressions of people who entered the room mirrored their anxiety, fear, suspicion, and resentment. After all, reorganizations mean change that might involve closed doors for some, new challenges for others, and different relationships among staff members. People walk into such meetings wondering who is going to get more, who will get less.

At one end of the room sat the president and two vice-presidents, one of whom explained the rationale for the reorganization, the new reporting lines, and the shuffling of responsibilities. He opened the floor up for questions.

In a voice that was shaky from tension and anger, one long-term employee expressed his opposition to some of the changes and to the fact that the plan was presented to the staff as a *fait accompli*. He talked for more than five minutes. When he was finished, he was addressed by the president, who repeated in outline form what the v.p. had already said.

Other employees voiced concerns or asked questions that reflected anxiety. Each time a rational, factual answer was given. The executives were tense, no question about it. But they never lost their cool.

I had an opportunity to talk privately with employees after the meeting. Listening to the outpouring of complaints about the meeting, I realized that the corporate executives had, if anything, increased the dissatisfaction and raised the level of tension and anger. They had certainly not resolved any of the negative feelings. And a tremendous amount of energy was consumed in the informal meetings after the meeting.

This kind of meeting is an executive's nightmare. Perhaps the saddest fact is that the president and his two associates were not aware of the prolonged negative feelings that came out of the meeting. Even if these men had chosen the best options in the planned reorganization and did a good job in explaining and detailing them, there was one area in which they did a terrible job. They refused to acknowledge that the people in the room had feelings.

Oftentimes people refuse to acknowledge the feelings of others because they don't know how to deal with those feelings. We know they're there, but we pretend that they're not. Sometimes you can see managers getting uptight, even blustery, when confronted with feelings. They seem to be saying, "You have no right to clutter up this discussion with your feelings."

Granted, it is not easy to deal with feelings. But it is certainly difficult to get anything accomplished without dealing with them. Feelings such as those present in the reorganization meeting will go underground to surface in any number of bitter springs later—low morale, lack of commitment, subversion, and resistance to management.

One way to start dealing with feelings is to admit that they are there. The president could have said, "These are the reasons why we have chosen this route. But I know that some of you are wondering just how these changes will affect you. You may be a little anxious, probably uncertain. I wish I had all the answers to put everyone at ease. I wish I could assure everyone that no one will be disadvantaged by these changes. I can't. We believe we've made the best decisions, but there is no such thing in the organizational world as certainty before the fact. You see, we have our anxious feelings, too. But if you'd like to talk about yours, we promise to listen. If you'd like to talk privately, our offices are available. Maybe we can all air our hopes and fears and work to make this change everything that we believe it can be."

That is a very human statement. It accepts the fact that people in the room are concerned. It even might suggest that the decisions are not all cast in concrete, that some accommodations, even if minor ones, might be made. At any rate, there will be sympathetic listening available.

There are times when the best you can do is to offer to listen. What you are conveying is, "Look, I know you have strong feelings. There may be nothing I can do about them. But I'm willing to listen and to give you a chance to express them." You might be surprised to find out how very much just listening means to the other person.

In addition to acknowledging people's feelings and being a ready, sympathetic listener, there are other things you can do to help both of you:

Be ready for the inevitable emotional reaction

The person affected is going to feel shock, bitterness, resentment. And he or she may not spare *your* feelings by hiding behind a stiff upper lip. Whatever people in this kind of traumatic situation say, or think to themselves, they will not be ready to listen to your reasoned explanation until they have expressed their emotions or had time to swallow the hurt. After you have allowed them that time, then:

Give a straight, unembellished explanation

Describe the circumstances that led to the decision. But keep it succinct. People who have heard bad news are not ready to listen to long explanations, because they are absorbed in their own problems. And if they hear a lengthy, involved story, they often think they're being snowed.

Sell the benefits of acceptance

To a person who is being fired, for example, offer the use of a telephone or office for a reasonable period and duplicating facilities for a resume. If you have suggestions for a job search, make them. Emphasize that time cannot be wasted: the sooner the person organizes a job-hunting campaign, the better off he or she will be.

Offer your help in making the adjustment

You can listen, offer advice, refer the person to other help. You cannot change the circumstances, but you can offer to help the person get through them, perhaps even find an opportunity in them.

People who are hurt by a decision also suffer a sudden, intense loss of self-esteem. Whatever actions you take along the above lines show that you understand that. Your willingness to reach out to them puts a more human face on management at a time when an impersonal approach (often simpler for the manager to take) would make the bad news even harder to bear.

The three most important things you can do during an interview in which you describe a change that is bad news for another are:

1. Be straight with the facts.

2. Emphasize the finality of the change and the need to get on with the necessary steps.

3. Accept the other person's feelings.

Turning down a raise request

When a subordinate asks for a well-earned pay increase that you must deny for some good reason, a simple "No" always sounds too harsh. But since that is exactly what you have to say, how do you say it?

Say it simply and directly

Express yourself along the lines of "I'd like to, but I can't. There just isn't the money." The employee may try to get you to add something, or you, eager to keep your subordinate happy, may be tempted to hold out hope. But this will muddle your message and may weaken your credibility with your employee.

Maintain your credibility

It may seem harmless to say, "When next month's sales figures are in, I'll reconsider" or "The boss may be in a better mood after we renegotiate that contract." But unless you are certain the picture will change, such replies merely keep the pay issue alive when you would be better off putting an end to it. If you hold out hopes for the future, you may only end up having to turn down the request a second time, at which point the subordinate may tag you as evasive or undependable.

Explain as much as is necessary

Offer an explanation, yes—but be wary of sounding apologetic. Mention the facts behind the decision, making it clear that it is those *facts* you regret. For example, in giving your reasons for the turndown, it is best to avoid a statement like, "I'd give you the raise, but my boss won't let me." Even if it is true, the person hearing it may think you're passing the buck or that you made an ineffective case. Saying "I have been told that all salary increases are frozen for the next quarter. I wish I had the power to make an exception, but I don't," is factual, sympathetic, and firm.

Expect your explanation to be accepted

There is no reason to prepare yourself for a big argument. A subordinate who asks for a raise will often be content to show dissatisfaction with the current salary. Having made the point, and received assurance that an increase is deserved, the subordinate may drop the subject.

Let the person go over your head, if necessary

If the employee is not satisfied with what you are selling him, let him speak to a higher-up. The employee will feel better having given a good, if unsuccessful, try. So don't discourage a request to speak to the executive you report to, even if you're sure it's futile.

Since you will probably never have enough money to satisfy everyone, this is a good time to consider other ways of recognizing your subordinate's performance—anything from a business trip to a new and closer working relationship with you. Let the person know that it is a reward, the only one you are able to give right now, so that it does not come across as an attempt to soothe his disappointment. And pick something that you know the subordinate will value.

These recommendations are equally useful when you turn an employee down on a raise that you do not think is deserved. However, in such a case, your regret is that the employee does not perform to your satisfaction. And you do not need to apologize for your decision.

Denying a promotion

"I want to apply for that job as expediting manager."

He stands there in your office, confident and resolute. He is a good worker, smart and skillful. But a manager? In expediting? That's a job that calls for tact. He tends to be brusque. In fact, his abrasiveness has already created problems for you.

How do you tell this good employee that you really think he would make a poor manager? Of course, you could always let him think you were considering him, but that will lead to unrealistic expectations. And when the expectations are disappointed, he is bound to feel resentment and be less eager to keep up the good work in a job he *can* handle.

Yet he isn't going to like your telling him that he is not, in your judgment, qualified for management. He is a good performer, and you would like to let him down as gently as possible.

First consideration: You do not have to give any answer immediately. Obviously there are reasons he wants this particular job. Asking him to talk about them is a good idea.

Second consideration: This is a learning opportunity for you. If you want to know what motivates this employee, there is no better chance than now.

Third consideration: One reason this employee does not see that he is unsuitable is that either you have not done enough coaching or what you have done didn't take. Your job is to coach employees on the job to help them grow and develop greater effectiveness, and you need to help them see in what direction that growth will take place. So this employee's unrealistic ambition is an indicator of where you haven't done as thorough a coaching job as needed and where improvements can be made.

But now he is sitting there, telling you all the reasons he is interested in this job. And what do you do? Remember that a good salesperson doesn't always sell what the prospect wants but rather what the salesperson thinks is right for that prospect's needs. So, as you listen, look for hopes and expectations that could be met some other way. It is possible, for example, that the employee is not overwhelmingly set on managing, but just wants a change, an opportunity to do something new.

But if the enthusiasm for the promotion is unwavering, you have to level with him: "Look, Jim, that particular job isn't for you. One of the main requirements of an expediting manager is the ability to get along with *everybody*. It's my observation that you've had trouble in that area in the past."

At this point, don't pause for agreement, because you could get an argument instead. Go on smoothly. "But it's plain to me you want to go further, make more money, have more challenge. I think we ought to talk about that and how to get you ready for it."

Right then, start developing a plan of growth and action, a new product. How can the employee become more skilled in other areas of interest? What goals would be realistic? How can they be achieved? This is your chance to provide the coaching that evidently has been deficient.

If the employee insists upon being considered for management eventually, then spell out the skills that he will have to develop. In Jim's case you might say, "How the people you work with and who report to you *see* you is very important to a manager's effectiveness. For example, I would guess that many feel that you're impatient and short-tempered. That's what I hear, anyway. Is that your view?"

Then, "What I'm getting at is that, to succeed as a manager, you'd have to convince people that you want to develop other people, that you not only want good results from them now but even better performance in the future, and that you are willing to work with them to help them become more valuable in the organization. Learning how to do that will certainly take time and patience. But if, after thinking it over, you're absolutely certain that's the way you'd like to go, I'm willing to help you develop those managerial skills."

With words like those, your example alone will illustrate the time and patience it takes to be a good manager. After that, it's up to Jim to change his style—or his ambitions.

In both of the above examples, you can recognize how this problem can be turned into an opportunity—one step backward and two forward. You can also see that there are times when you are approached as a buyer and exchange roles. You become a seller instead.

Encouraging behavior changes

Many managers have some grounding in psychology that they put to good use on the job. But no manager should attempt to be a therapist. Being a good salesperson will do, even when it comes to counseling employees in ways to be more effective on the job or helping them to alter the way they do things. Most people are agreeable to changing their behavior when it makes sense to them and when it will bring rewards. But they often need to be sold on the changes.

Techniques for changing behavior that both managers and subordinates can accept have to be open, agreed to. They must *not* be manipulative—in other words, they should be based on good selling. For example, Tony Howard is a highly motivated, inventive, generally effective manager. Everyone agrees he shows a high degree of personal security, with one exception: In meetings when his ideas are questioned or criticized, Tony talks, and talks, and talks. He cuts off the critics, trying to anticipate their objections. He rambles. His frustration becomes obvious as he fails to respond to what people are asking. The others become irritated and querulous.

His boss, Peter Tappan, considers that Tony would be more effective, that he would have more ideas accepted, and certainly more cooperation in implementing them, if he would calm down and listen better. Peter wants to work with Tony in making behavioral changes that would help Tony get better results. Here are the techniques he uses:

Choosing the right time

A subordinate who has just gone through a rough, frustrating experience is usually ready to talk about a different way of doing things. When Tony has experienced an especially frustrating meeting, Peter looks for the sign that he is ready for something that will help him avoid more of the same in the future.

Unfortunately, managers, being human, sometimes urge a behavioral change after what has been a disappointing experience for *them*. The employee has been embarrassing, goofed terribly. The manager is upset and chooses that time to lay it on. The employee resists buying. Unless the employee clearly expresses or seems to recognize a need to do *something now*, it is advisable to wait until the subordinate is more receptive.

However, even when the subordinate doesn't see the need for a change, the manager may be able to do a good selling job by supplying information that the subordinate doesn't have. To illustrate: "I have to tell you that as a result of the way you talked to that employee, a grievance has been filed. It's going to cost us a lot of time and trouble."

Many managers prefer to discuss behavioral objectives during periodic coaching sessions to avoid the implication of you-and-I-had-better-talk-because-you-screwed-up. The message is clearly "I want to do what I can to help you be more effective all around." It is less threatening. Then manager and subordinate explore ways to do this and set behavioral objectives along with other goals.

Getting an agreement

On occasion, you may have coached someone in a change that makes sense to you and then wondered why it didn't take hold. If an employee is to agree to a change in behavior, the new behavior has to be important and feasible to that person, not merely to you. (Remember, be assertive *and* responsive.)

Peter talks to Tony about what he has observed without loading on too much criticism. He dwells on what he has seen—the reactions of others around the table, the wasted time and energy, the poor results. Peter is concerned with making a case, but no more than that. Tony nods and says, "Yes, I know I blab a lot. But sometimes I can't believe the kind of stuff I hear."

Peter suggests (I repeat, *suggests*) that Tony might hear quite different things if he spent a bit more time listening carefully before answering or defending. He describes the consequences of a change of behavior as a benefit. Tony agrees that might be true. He is willing to give it a try.

Focusing on behavior

Attitudes are hard to deal with. "I wish you would try to be less defensive" is not only putting a label on someone else's behavior, as well as labeling the motivation for it, but is sure to increase whatever defensiveness is there. So Peter makes a concrete proposal. He asks Tony to wait a certain interval before answering any objections. Here is how he defines the behavior that he wants in Tony: "If someone asks you for clarification, by all means answer. But if someone voices an opinion that may be different from your own, I'd like you to experiment with sitting there for a full fifteen seconds without saying a word."

He explains that at least two things may occur in that period. One, someone else may respond to the criticism or provide answers. Two, Tony may find that what he thought he had heard was not really what the other person meant.

Salespeople, you'll remember, know the value of not jumping to meet the first objection to the sale. Peter is asking Tony to pause for the same reason. Tony agrees to try.

Incidentally, Peter may suggest they role-play. Tony would offer an idea as if he were in a meeting. Peter could respond with questions or criticism. The two of them could then work on specific appropriate behaviors for Tony.

Recognizing the change

The best feedback comes from success in trying the new behavior. It might not come at the first attempt, or, if it does, it might not be recognized as such by the subordinate. That's why your reinforcement is so important. It answers the question in the subordinate's mind, "Am I really doing it the way we agreed?"

If Tony's behavior, in waiting, seemed to be successful—if, that is, it resulted in more constructive interaction around the table—then Peter's feedback is very important, since Tony may not have been able right away to see the successful results. And the feedback and reinforcement should continue until the new behavior is well-established.

Managers are often heard to say things like, "But can't he see. . . ?" or "Doesn't she realize. . . ?" Whether it is inappropriate or self-defeating or something that should be done but isn't, it is usually true that, no, the employee does *not* realize what is happening. Whatever he or she is doing may, in that person's mind, be the best solution. So it is up to the manager to coach the subordinate in becoming more effective by finding a better way. Employees have a right to expect that from their bosses.

Coping with employee defensiveness

One form of resistance that managers often run into in trying to correct a subordinate's ineffective or below-standard performance is the employee's defensiveness. This difficulty can be especially acute with people who have supervisory responsibilities. They are likely to be intensely sensitive to any criticism, real or implied, that reflects on their competence in your eyes and in those of their subordinates.

Defensiveness can destroy any attempt to get the employee to acknowledge the problem and agree to an effective solution. While it cannot be eliminated entirely, you can control it by maintaining an atmosphere of helpfulness and by avoiding personal criticism. Here are some methods to try:

Get right to the point

Bring the bottom line up to the top. It is tempting to open a performance counseling session with idle pleasantries. The subordinate, however, is probably expecting you to get to the problem. Consequently, any delay will only increase anxiety about what you have to say.

State the problem without evaluating it

Start by describing specific evidence of a problem: "Your group's rejection rate has been about 10 percent above standard for the past three weeks." Do *not* ask why or demand to know what the subordinate is going to do about it. Rather, sit back for a few moments and wait for a response to your statement.

Avoid arguing with the explanation given

The employee's immediate reaction is likely to be self-justification. If you argue or try to make suggestions at this point, you may only provoke further self-justification. Instead, echo the explanations in simple declarative form. This will encourage your subordinate to get to the real root of the problem, which you, after all, may not be aware of. Say, for example, "You think the new equipment is the source of the trouble," or "You feel the standards are unrealistic." This should keep the discussion moving.

It may also be necessary to encourage the employee's analysis of the problems by asking occasional questions. But remember, "how" questions tend to foster cooperation, while "why" questions generally tend to foster defensiveness. So ask, "How can we solve it?" not "Why did it happen?"

Restate the importance of the person's work goals, then ask about the solution

"I recognize your problems, Lee, but the unit can't afford this much waste. How can we get back into line with quality goals?" Most likely, the subordinate will stop worrying about your assessment of him or her and start thinking about a solution: "Let me call the salesperson who sold us that machine and see whether he can help."

Once you've arrived at a solution, sum up the situation yourself or have the employee do so. That way, there will be no misunderstanding about what has to be done. It is also a good idea to make arrangements for a follow-up meeting or at least to check back later to make sure no further problems have been encountered.

Maintaining control

The essence of success in selling bad news is control. From the outset you control the interview. You never abdicate your role as the persuader. As you know, that does not mean that you are not responsive to the other person. In fact, you must be responsive. You will usually get much less resistance when your listener believes that you are concerned with his or her needs, his or her feelings.

When you are engaged in a painful, embarrassing interview, listening becomes harder than ever. The temptation is strong to talk, talk, and to talk some more. If you talk, you don't have to listen. If you listen, you may hear thoughts and feelings that will increase your discomfort. But you cannot hope to get acceptance of your bad news unless you involve the other person and show by that involvement that you have confidence in what you are doing. You may not be liked, but you will be trusted and respected.

Selling bad news to the boss

When you have bad news to give to the boss, the same selling techniques apply as when you talk with subordinates. Except, of course, delivering bad news to the boss can be even more painful, especially when you may be the cause of the mishap. Assume, for example, that you have been handed an important assignment, a survey, that you have in turn delegated to a usually capable subordinate. Her work comes back to you by the deadline, but to your distress, it is not what the boss wants from you. In your discussion with the employee, you realize that your instructions to her were misleading. There is no time to do it over. You believe that you have no option except to tell the boss about the mess. There is no way to escape the pain, but you can make it less traumatic for both you and the boss by following these recommendations:

Choose the occasion

As you have seen, this is fundamental in selling, and it is especially important when you have to unload unpleasantness. Let the boss know that you have something to discuss that requires time and quiet. You do not want to be interrupted during this interview, so emphasize the seriousness of your request without getting too much into the substance. Giving bad news to the boss while he or she is busy at something else could be inflammable. Decline, if you can get away with it, to provide the details until you have your private time. But don't delay too long. Urge the boss to grant you an early session, no matter how busy his or her schedule is.

Come right to the point

Good news or bad, this is essential advice. You cannot be blamed for wanting to give a long preamble before you get to the point, but stalling only worsens the situation. The tension will build in the boss who is wondering what you are leading up to. Another temptation to avoid is digging up some good news to try to soften the blow. No one likes to be lifted up, only to be dropped. Besides, if the good news is genuinely good, you're throwing it away. It will be thoroughly spoiled by any bad news that follows.

Accept the responsibility

Although your subordinate misunderstood your instructions, assume that you are the one to blame. You should have made certain that she understood clearly. You didn't, so the responsibility rests on your shoulder. You don't have to flagellate yourself; just quietly let the boss know that you know where the responsibility lies. Move on quickly from here.

Have an action plan

Yes, you messed up, but your accepting responsibility doesn't get the job done. So how can you do it? You might suggest putting several of your subordinates on the project on a crash basis. Perhaps a few people working overtime could clean it up. If possible, present a plan, listing the resources you would need and a time frame for its accomplishment. Everyone makes mistakes, but not everyone seems to be able to develop a plan for correction.

Get the boss's approval to the plan

Whatever you come up with as a plan—your own or the boss's or one worked out jointly—close on it. You do not want to leave anything hanging. If you do, the boss might give the plan to someone else to do, and you will be left with the mud while someone else gets the garland.

In selling any kind of bad news, a fundamental consideration is your preservation of credibility. Your message is, "This is what has happened. I take responsibility for it (or, I stand behind it)." The person who waffles on responsibility or wavers in support of the decision risks losing credibility. An equally vital attitude to maintain is the one that says, "All right, this is the way it is. Now what can we do about it?" The person who assumes full responsibility for a bad situation *and* can answer "What can we do about it?" can sell bad news to the boss and even come out ahead of the game.

10

Selling to a Group

You are the planning director of a medium-size company, well-established in its field. Your company offers three product lines. The A line consists of manually operated tools and equipment that rese.nble, and in some cases *are*, the original products of the company during its formative years in the early 1920s. Product line B is second generation: electrically operated tools and machinery. Line C is fairly new and consists of highly sophisticated equipment that is controlled by small computers.

You have held your position less than a year, but during that time you have become convinced that greater effort should be applied to line C. Not only are you convinced that the marketing opportunities are tremendous, but, because the field has not yet become crowded with competitors, you can show that the profit-per-sale is impressive. You foresee that your company has an opportunity to become a leader in the field of computer-operated equipment.

The volume of line B is large, and the profit margins are respectable. You see no reason to reduce the marketing efforts there. But line A is traditional. The field is crowded. The profit margins are low, although the sales volume is large, due to customer loyalty to the company name.

You have a somewhat daring plan. You want to milk product line A. That is, you want to stop advertising and promotion of those products, and divert that money to developing the market for line C. You reason that, through the years, the sales of line A have reached a momentum that will continue without much additional thrust by the company. You want to turn over all sales of line A products to distributors.

Your boss is intrigued by your proposal. You have practiced your sales presentation on him. He wants time to think. When you next hear from him, the word is that he has arranged a meeting. You are to give a presentation to a group consisting of the chairman of the board, the president, the executive vice-president, your boss, the treasurer, the national sales manager, and other executives.

Your first reaction to the message is ambivalent. You are pleased that your boss has taken you seriously and has arranged a forum in which you can sell your ideas. However, you have anxious feelings about giving a presentation to such a group.

Advantages of a group presentation

It is safe to say that *most* people have a problem giving a talk or a presentation to a group of people. Their hands tremble, their throats go dry, they worry about their minds going blank. What if they make fools of themselves, they wonder.

There is no getting around it—making a presentation to a group of people is usually more tension-producing than talking to one person. It is often much easier to establish rapport with one person, and it is certainly easier to get a conversation going with one person than with several. You have less control over a group. They can influence one another, especially if they are acquaintances or co-workers, more readily than you can influence them. Too, there is a self-consciousness, or stiffness, among people in groups. Interestingly, they may be just as uncomfortable as you are, and if you feel resistance from them, it may stem from that discomfort.

But on the plus side, talking to or persuading a group can provide a real high. When you realize that what you say and how you say it have been successful at breaking down the barriers between you, that people are talking to you and asking questions, and discussing your proposal among themselves, you feel a strong sense of achievement, even power.

Aside from ego and a test of your skills, presenting to a group offers you several advantages:

- A group presentation can save you an enormous amount of time in reaching the many people who may possibly influence the decision.
- It assures you that each of the people involved in the decision will each receive exactly the same story.
- Having the influentials gathered together provides you with the opportunity to ask questions, flush out objections, and get agreement on needs.
- Finally, it provides you important allies in those people who express approval of your proposal or aspects of it. These allies can help sway the rest of the group—often better than you can.

Marshaling your support

In addition to your verbal presentation, you will want to have certain kinds of back up support to reinforce what you are saying and expand on it.

Have supporting facts on hand

You never know when a committee member will want more data or authority for what you say. So it is essential to be armed with twice as much ammunition as you are likely to use. Have it well organized so that you can quickly find what you need.

Reinforce your message with visuals

Visual aids heighten interest in your presentation if only because more than one sense is being appealed to. They reinforce the verbal message. You may wish to have charts showing volume vs. profit for lines A, B, and C. Another chart would show actual and projected growth for line C. An effective visual could be as simple as a blow-up of a full-page magazine advertisement. The important thing is that the visuals are uncomplicated and easy to see.

Provide back-up material

Committee members will not remember all the points you will make. Therefore, consider handing out a synopsis or written proposal at the end of the meeting. If you hand it out before, they may read it while you are talking. You may want to use a special folder or binder complete with sketches, photos, or other visuals.

Formal vs. informal

Your approach to the group may be informal and low key, or you may wish to be more formal and dramatic. Either way, your approach should be matched to the needs of the group.

The formal approach works well with larger groups where you are confined to a lectern or a table at the front of the room. You may wish to make important points using a blackboard or another visual aid in your presentation. But there will be both a physical and psychological distance which you may never quite overcome.

The informal approach lets you get better acquainted more quickly when the group is small and friendly and allows a freer give-and-take by encouraging dialogue and interplay of personalities. You may prefer to sit among the other members of the group.

Though both of these approaches are effective and traditional, you should give some thought to occasionally switching your tactics, given the right mix of people and circumstances. If your information will not be all that new and astonishing, the *character* of your presentation might be the most impressive thing about it, and people in a large and formal gathering might be quite favorably impressed because you are different—because you walked around the room, inviting questions, establishing dialogues here and there between participants, asking your own questions, and so on.

Wherever you locate yourself, choose a place where you can see peoples' faces. Not only do you enhance your presentation with eye contact, but you also need to watch faces to see how people are responding to your ideas or whether they are hearing you. You will also want to spot those who are potential allies and influentials.

Bringing help

In presenting to a group, you will want to consider the possibility of a back-up team, anyone, in fact, who could add interest, authority, knowledge, or professionalism to your presentation. If you plan to use this type of assistance, choose people who are articulate and at ease with the group. All the technical knowledge in the world will not impress, coming from an individual who is nervous, embarrassed, or uncomfortable.

Be sure to discuss your role and theirs ahead of time so that there is no mixup or confusion during the actual presentation. Someone has to be in charge, and that is you.

When you begin your presentation, introduce your team to the group, and explain how it will help you and benefit your audience. In addition to name and title, highlight specific areas of expertise: "Jim Holly is our expert on unitized shipments."

If you work as a well-coordinated team, you will come across as organized, efficient, and effective.

Preparing for the presentation

Not only do you need to know who will be at the meeting, you need to get some idea as to where each person is likely to stand on the issue of milking line A and pushing line C. For example, the chairman is the son of the company's founder. Will he be tied to the old products by sentiment? Will the national sales manager anticipate trouble with the field sales force by switching entirely to distributors on line A?

These are questions and potential problems that need to be anticipated. Your boss is a good resource. Find out how he or she sees the divergence of views and the possible partisanship. If some members of the group will confide in you, tap their opinions.

You can never give a sales presentation without experiencing a surprise or two. Your objective is to limit those surprises to the lowest possible number. Get to know your prospects. What's more, get to know how your prospects will relate to one another in the meeting. Who will be deferential to whom? Who will influence, or be influenced by, whom?

The presentation

Since you are a junior member of the group, you might get a boost by having your boss introduce you. Not a formal introduction, of course, since presumably everyone at the meeting knows you, but your boss can act as a sponsor, even a buffer. (After all, one of the most important roles a manager can play is protector of subordinates.) Your boss can explain that you came to him with an intriguing, imaginative idea, that he felt it was worthy of high-level consideration, and that he will turn the meeting over to you so that you can give your presentation.

Whether you present to a large group or small, a group that is made up of strangers or co-workers, it is important to make sure that they know exactly why you are there and what role you are playing. Do not even assume that your co-workers know what you are about to do or what is expected of them. If you can't get an introduction from another, do the explaining yourself.

As you take control, remember: Don't keep them waiting for the reasons why they are there. Let your excitement show a bit. "Over the past six months I've been doing substantial research into our markets and profits, and I'm now convinced that we have created a beachhead in a market that can increase our sales volume in the next five years by about 500 percent and our profits by nearly 800 percent."

How's that for a grabber? You are going to increase volume impressively and profits tremendously. "I'm also convinced that most of the costs of developing this marketing strategy can be covered by cash that we generate through our present selling efforts. And I'd like to explain how this can be done."

(If you don't have their attention now, you really do have an uphill campaign.)

How long should your presentation be? Most people do not have a lengthy span of concentration. Sixty to ninety minutes for the whole session is tolerable. A rule of thumb is that your prepared presentation should take up about half of that. That means something like thirty to forty minutes for your presentation. Let your visuals do some of the work. If you have uncovered some objections, you might want to include some answers to them in your presentation. However, it is not usually a good idea to try to anticipate every objection. If they haven't thought of it, there is no point in your putting it in their minds.

As you talk, you will probably sense that you are building a good rapport with one or more members of the group. He smiles and nods in agreement. You receive lots of eye contact. It is tempting to direct much of your presentation to that seeming ally. A friendly face is a pleasant audience. But if you concentrate your attention on the nodder, you risk excluding others, possibly even alienating them with your excessive concern for the one member of the group. Everyone wants and needs some eye contact from you. In addition, your concentration on one member may encourage others to suspect that he is no longer objective and will probably be partisan in the discussion. Thus you will have inadvertently weakened a potential ally.

Dealing with questions

In most presentations, whether before large and small groups, you want questions. They show interest, give you feedback, and help you expand your message. Should you encourage people in the group to bring up questions as you speak, or wait until the end of your presentation?

You might want to ask that questions be held until the end when time for your presentation is very short and you have much information to give or when the group is large and diverse, containing people of varying levels of knowledge and expertise. Questions can throw you off, and, when time is limited, they can prevent you from covering your subject. People will often become annoyed when you cut short your coverage.

You might want to hear questions as they come up but not necessarily answer them right away. Many experienced presenters dislike having to ignore questions because questions tell them when they're getting through to people, and when their presentation is not clear or comprehensible.

If the question refers to material that you are sure you will cover, ask the questioner to hold it until you come to that part of the presentation. If the question reflects a distinctly minority interest or is germane to one person, ask that it be held until the end or taken up with you individually afterward. If the question requires a lengthy answer that might disrupt the timetable, explain why you cannot do justice to it at the time and offer to cover it if there is time at the end.

Some questions are tough, even hostile. You get the clear message that the questioner is not sympathetic with your position. Some queries will cause you to feel vulnerable to attack—and you are, if you let yourself be. When you encounter this kind of antagonism, you can expect to be upset. At such momemts, it is easy to depart from the rational and make a careless or retaliatory remark. To guard against weakening your case in that way, follow these guidelines:

Be open and honest

The statement may be thrown at you like a dart: "What you are really saying is that because of sloppy management, overall production fell off sharply in your department in 1981." Placed in such an unfavorable spot, you may be tempted to try to win over the audience or pacify the questioner's negative feelings. But you are going after respect, not affection, and respect usually comes from a display of honesty.

Don't fudge the issue with, "Well, actually, you'll observe that output per person starting in September was higher than any previous period and that means that. . . ." No one is likely to be fooled by that subterfuge. Instead, say: "The answer to that is, yes, we fell below last year. And there are a number of reasons for that decline, which I'll be glad to spell out for you. But I'm not ready to agree with the sloppy management diagnosis."

Go for wide participation

One very negative person can continue to ask questions. When you get too many questions from one person, say, "I would like to answer other people's questions, too. If there's time afterward, I'll be glad to come back to you." If you don't open the floor to others, you will find yourself in a possible no-win debate with the one person who may have come prepared to do you in.

Show your critics respect

Especially in a large group, obnoxious questioners may tempt you to score at their expense. For example, one speaker spotted an unsupportable statement in an abrasive comment by a woman in the audience. He gave a devastating answer consisting of five points that proved her wrong. Before each point, he repeated her statement sarcastically. He won the argument—but lost the audience.

You are at the lectern. You have rehearsed. You have an advantage. The other person is speaking extemporaneously and appears to be at a disadvantage. So don't try to widen the gap. Your respect for a questioner, especially one who has baited you, will win respect for *you*.

Handling the devil's advocate

A word about a phenomenon in some organizations: the professional devil's advocate. There are some people who seem to be perennial nay-sayers. You can often identify this person by his or her repeated use of "yes, but. . ." "This plan sounds like a good idea, but we tried something like this in our department and it didn't work." Or, "It's very logical, but some of the people who will carry it out aren't." The nay-sayer is very smooth at giving with one hand and taking away with the other.

One of the most impressive "no" people I've ever met always spoke in a lower register, which imparts weight to the words. He spoke slowly and thoughtfully. He was very self-assured and articulate. His colleagues told me his function was to tell you that your ideas wouldn't work and why. His boss apparently found him quite indispensable when he himself didn't want to appear negative, or when he wasn't clear what stand he should take. He brought along solemn old Fred to take a stand for him.

Try to avoid a direct confrontation with the nay-sayer. He is probably very good at what he does, and he has to maintain his reputation. If you press him, you will force him to use all of his skills. My experience is that few challengers win. They find themselves playing in the other person's ballpark. Do not give the devil's advocate prominence in the group. Listen and avoid arguing, if you can. Others in the group will come to recognize where this fellow is coming from.

Using questions for control

A group will be slower to understand you than an individual; that is, people learn at different rates of speed, and with several people present you must wait until *all* have reached understanding before you can leave an issue. Ongoing, continual understanding of what you are saying is crucial in a group presentation. Usually, if it is proceeding well and is intriguing to your listeners, questions will arise naturally.

If there is no response—no questions, not a word or glance exchanged between members of the group—you can be certain that something is awry. Chances are, your presentation is not stimulating thought, or it's going over their heads. Either way, it is dangerous.

Pause for a moment, address your own question to someone, or pose a question to answer yourself. If you suspect people are bored, check. For example, "Is there any need to spend more time on this? Or should I move faster to the next point?" What you hope is that you will get either a question or a signal to move on.

Don't be in a rush to answer a question or objection. Instead, pause for a moment and really *ponder* your answer. It appears more dramatic and thought-provoking, whether you need the time to think or not: "Mrs. Horvath, that's a good question. . . *(pause)* . . . the reason is . . ." Pausing is respectful. You want to encourage their feeling of self-importance and incisiveness, not put them down.

If you need time to think, repeat the question, checking with the questioner to make sure you have it right. This is a technique that should always be used in a large group where the acoustics are uncertain. It is entirely possible that someone in the group will be willing, even eager, to answer the objection or question. You need only sit back, hold your fire, and let the other person do your selling. He or she will give the impression of being more objective than you, however candid you may try to be. In addition, the feeling of participation will reach out to group members and begin to affect them more subtly, but more deeply, than you could hope to. As soon as the point has been made, when you sense that no one else will add anything, nod in agreement to the statement, thank the replier, and continue.

After the presentation

You have made your presentation, verbally and on paper. Now it is time for other members of the group to discuss your proposal. It may be a tense time for you. After all, a lot is at stake—the ideas themselves, the esteem of others, your prestige, your reputation, your standing in the group. It is a crucial time for you, a time when you can very easily undo all of the good you have accomplished so far. No matter how valid the ideas, no matter how impressive the presentation, you can foul it all up in the group discussion that follows.

How? By talking too much.

You've been center stage. You've done your act. Now it's time to get your audience more involved. If you don't, they cannot and will not take action. And the repeated sound of your voice will either bore or anger them.

Furthermore, by talking too much, you might appear defensive and unsure. Presumably you have given your colleagues the good reasons why they should accept what you have given them. But if you talk at every opportunity, show nervousness, react to opposition or questioning with irritation, then you broadcast some unfortunate messages—that you don't trust either your reasons or your colleagues. Undoubtedly you have sat in a meeting with a colleague who was reacting to stress in these ways and you have probably wanted to pull him aside and say, "For heaven's sake, shut up."

At some point you have to begin to trust the idea, yourself, and your co-workers. If you are confident that the idea makes sense, then you have to give it time to settle in. As for you, you have had your time. Granted, you aren't finished yet, but the greater part of your opportunity to influence has passed. (If the prospect has not been partly sold by the presentation, he or she probably will not be persuaded by even the most brilliant post-presentation tactics.) Your co-workers need time to flex their mental muscles and process what you have said.

A third reason you don't want to talk too much is that you might, without being aware of it, provide others with a reason not to buy. For example, if you have not discussed the fact that your proposal would require the immediate hiring of two specialized salespeople, someone will probably bring it up. It is possible that someone else will suggest that the hiring can be offset by the impending retirement of an older highly paid salesperson. Before that happens, you jump in and say, "Well, I carefully considered the pros and cons of that. At most, it might involve an immediate outlay of about $30,000 and it didn't seem to me to be something to worry about." Of course not—not to you, the originator of the change. But now someone will say, "Maybe it's something that we ought to worry about."

Remember the old war poster, "Loose lips sink ships"? They sink sales, too. By talking more than you need to, you may bring up problems that otherwise would not have surfaced. Years ago, as a young salesman, I made a presentation to the president of a medium-size company. The program I was selling consisted of printed material and came in multiple units. This executive wanted to buy just one. I told him I couldn't do that. He asked why. I could have said that was company policy based on cost consideration. But he was a nice person, and I thought we had good rapport. So I told him about another company, a large corporation, that had bought one unit and duplicated it in-house. That's why we had imposed the policy.

His facial muscles became taut as he said, "I have no intention of trying to steal anything from you." I didn't get the sale; I didn't deserve it. I talked too much.

The better you know your colleagues, the friendlier you all are, the easier it is to forget that your words may be used against you. They could provide someone with a reason to say no.

While you might see yourself as primarily passive during this post-presentation period, there are several things you can and should be doing:

1. Listen actively

This is another reason for not talking much. If you are trying to think of the right things to say, you are not listening well. Here are some of the things you are listening for:

What are the strengths that others see in your plan? You are fortunate if people talk about the pluses that they see in your proposal. And their pluses may be different from those you think are critical.

What are the weaknesses that they see, and how serious are they? Is your perception of a flaw shared by others? People who do not listen well may find themselves consuming precious time rebutting a point that other people don't take seriously anyway. It was never a major sticking point, except in the presenter's mind.

Who seems to be lining up on what side? Who expresses serious

and repeated opposition? Those are important qualifying words—
serious, repeated. Remember that some people will bring up their
reservations not because they regard them as serious but because
they feel a need to say something, or to appear objective. If they do
not repeat their reservations, you can often write them off. Look for
your supporters, too, those who will be your base of strength.

Who seems to be uncommitted? Silence does not necessarily
mean neutrality or objective detachment. The person who is quiet
may still be making up his or her mind, trying to determine where
the power centers are, or hoping not to have to reveal partisanship.

Where are the subgroups forming? Who is influencing whom?
Politics, as well as the issues themselves, is involved. I recall one
meeting in which a proposal was being discussed, and I had been
told that one manager would be quite negative. And indeed he was.
But his boss was there, too. At one point the manager voiced another
one of his several objections. This time his boss replied that he did
not regard that objection as very important, and then he went on
to express cautious approval of the plan. All opposition from the
negative manager ceased. If the presenter had confronted the manager earlier, she might have become mired in fruitless discussion.
The person to concentrate on was the nay-sayer's boss. He was the
key to the manager's position.

2. Clarify

It's your proposal. You know it best. You are the group's primary
resource. So, answer questions put to you, but don't feel that you
have to answer *every* question. Remember that it is better if someone
else in the group answers it for you. So, when a question is raised,
be thoughtful for a moment before replying. Perhaps you won't
have to.

From time to time you may have to intervene when the discussion
has gone way off the track or when it is clear that there is misunderstanding of your ideas. You don't have to call attention to either.
You can say something like, "Someone was talking about the need

to hire additional personnel. I wanted to clarify that. According to the calculation I did when I was working up that proposal. . . ."

Don't be long-winded. Say just enough to make your point and no more.

3. Summarize

Summarizing is a good thing to do if you are a) frustrated because the discussion does not seem to be taking a discernible direction, b) feeling left out of the discussion, or c) looking for a way to push an on-going favorable discussion even harder.

Obviously, to summarize you don't break into a heated debate or an intense exchange of any sort. But there are natural lags in the rhythm of a conference that permit you to break in with, "Maybe it's a good time to sum up some of the things that have been said thus far." Then do so—and pray that you don't put words in someone's mouth that cause regurgitation. If someone says, "No, that's not quite what I meant," accept it. There is not much point to a prolonged No-I-didn't-Yes-you-did kind of thing. Besides, you may have succeeded in getting a vigorous discussion going again.

A good summary puts you in the picture in a constructive light. It reinforces any good trends, and it could warn that the conference is not heading anywhere or is getting polarized. The group members may have chosen up sides without being entirely aware of it. The repetition of arguments has served mainly to harden positions. A good summary will point out this danger.

A good summary provides an excellent opportunity for closure. "Those seem to be the principal points in favor of the proposal. May I get started on the preliminary steps such as working with field sales to prepare new distributor contracts for the A line?"

Getting action

In giving any presentation, no matter how informal, do not forget to close. You may be distracted by all of the give-and-take of group discussion, or you may feel somewhat overwhelmed by numbers. But you must never wind up a group presentation without getting some commitment.

What are you hoping to get? Further consideration for your plan and a follow-up meeting? A go-ahead now? Appointment of a committee? Reference to another group? Then make sure that you try to get as close to what you want as possible.

State it: "I'd like to start organizing the special work group now so that they can be functional by the first of March. Shall I go ahead on that basis?"

Be assumptive. Your seeming confidence may pull a divided group together. Chances are that the group will often be reluctant to initiate action without being prodded. You, as presenter, probably have more at stake than anyone else, and will have to provide the prodding. Usually you want to pin down the following:

1. What is the group's decision?
2. How is it to be carried out?
3. Who is responsible for carrying it out?
4. What is the timetable for implementation?

If the group can come to no decision, even when you ask for one, you will not want to let it go at that. Ask questions such as, "What has to happen before we can make a decision?" or, "What additional information do you need?" or, "What stands between us and a decision?" You are looking for specific information that can tip you off to what additional steps you need to take and what objections are not being expressed by members of the group. Your allies may come to your aid if you provide the initiative.

Push for a close on something, even if it is only the date for the follow-up discussion. Closure at this point is very important, not only for you, but for all the members of the group. If people leave the room feeling directionless, you may lose much of the momentum that you have built up. Closure, getting some kind of action, provides people with a sense of achievement and direction.

11

Building Influence in Meetings

If you would like to influence much of the decision-making in your organization and win people's gratitude and respect at the same time, work to improve your meetings skills. Surveys show that people in responsible positions in organizations spend from one-third to one-half of the working schedules in meetings. (Most important decisions are made by groups, or at least are attempted by them.) People find many of those meetings boring and time-wasting, as indeed they are. One reason is that leaders of meetings often don't lead. They don't know how.

What's more, most of the people who complain that they have to spend so much time in meetings have not been trained in meeting skills and in group dynamics. Consequently they flounder, get side-tracked, or stumble when faced with resistance from others. Riptides and crosscurrents are rife in meetings, even when the participants know each other well, and experienced managers often find themselves at the mercy of the forces operating in a group instead of at the helm, making the meeting work for them.

If you can make a meeting work, that is, achieve a significant objective acceptable to the group, then you will usually be regarded with respect. Most people do not want to sit around a table for hours without some kind of closure or achievement. But sit around is what they do, if there isn't a skilled person in the group who knows how to guide a group toward its goal. It takes training and practice to acquire those skills, but they are invaluable. Meetings called to solve problems or make decisions offer unequalled opportunities to influence others to accept your ideas. If you are effective in meetings, even the people who oppose your positions will respect you and like to work with you. They may even come to agree with many of your stands.

There is at least one other reason why you should look forward to meetings: visibility. Other people in the organization have a chance to see you in action. If some of those people are higher-level managers, so much the better.

Group roles

There are basically four useful roles that you can play in a group: formal leader, informal leader, participant, and processor-observer. The formal leader is the person who calls and runs the meeting, by virtue of rank or designation. Obviously the formal leader can wield a lot of influence.

As a participant, you can of course advance your ideas and solutions, but you will probably be only one of several people doing this. What you want is to create opportunities for yourself to get more attention for your ideas from other participants. You don't want to be just one of several, you want to be the one who is listened to most.

Therefore, if you want your ideas to be accepted, you should be prepared to take over the informal leadership. Informal leadership consists of advancing and arguing your ideas, suggesting directions in which the group can move, and exercising a host of other constructive functions. Obviously, people who understand how and when to assume leadership are usually more influential than their colleagues.

One of the ways in which you can assume leadership is through process-observing. The process is what is going on among the participants, often referred to as the dynamics of the group. Some people talk in terms of a group personality. For example, is the group characterized by a wariness, a lack of trust, attempted dominance by some, an encouragement of open expression, or attempts to block the effectiveness of various participants? Is the atmosphere productive, distracted, competitive, tense? Are the majority of the people evasive, argumentative, ineffective? Process has to do with the interaction of the people involved, as opposed to the content or subject of the meeting and the methodology that has been chosen for the discussion (the time limits, how voting will occur, etc.).

Process-observing is a valuable role and skill, because it often gives you a reason to intervene in what is going on, perhaps even to assume a temporary leadership role. Whatever your intervention, it usually provides an opportunity to exercise influence.

Here is a good example of how effective process-observing can be for you—and it is the kind of situation that you have undoubtedly encountered many times. In a meeting that you are attending, progress has been halted by an argument between two participants. On the face of it, they are arguing from opposite ends of the spectrum. They use different words that seem to represent differing concepts. The more they talk, the more vehement and repetitive they get. Other members of the group may join in; undoubtedly some of them have taken a stand with one or the other antagonist. They have become partisans, and they listen to what their side says. They are sufficiently biased that they no longer listen carefully to what the other side is saying.

The discussion for the moment is stalled. There is no forward movement. If you were to assume the role of processor-observer, you would try to avoid partisanship in order to listen to what is actually being said by both sides. The first thing you notice is that they keep saying the same things over and over. They may even interject personal remarks out of anger and frustration: "If you'd think about it carefully. . ." (obviously the other person is not thinking at all) or "How can you sit there. . ." (and be so stupid). Probably they are no longer dealing with the issues but are trying either to score points in a debate or simply to wear each other down. They each act as if they are engaged in a win-lose competition: I win, the other person loses. Actually, the whole group is in a no-win situation. Not only will the contention prevent the group from doing its business, but it will result in ill will that can be carried from the conference room to the outside—and back in again at a later meeting.

But now that you are listening, you are surprised to notice two things. First, they no longer seem clear as to the issues, and second, they use different words but are closer to agreement on some aspects than they realize. They are not listening to each other. If you had not listened carefully, you probably would not have observed what was really going on. And that is the crucial point: You must learn to stop periodically and ask yourself, "What is going on here right now?" That is processing. You can now speak up, pointing out the fuzziness of the issues, and summarize the points of apparent agreement. Your calm intervention may serve to get the meeting moving forward again.

Assuming informal leadership can provide opportunities for you to get right into the center of what is going on. As a participant, you might have an opinion, but you have to get in line to present it. If you have especially relevant knowledge or experience, however, you can assume some authority in the group. For a time, you perform as a leader, exercising some control, influencing the direction that the group is taking.

Processing gives you much the same kind of entry. You may break up a log jam. Or you may sense that the group is beginning to move in one direction too fast and too soon, so you point this out and suggest that other options be considered (your own, for instance). Processing can open the door for you to exercise control and leadership. You have been a silent member. You become a vocal mover.

The beauty of knowing how and when to process and when to assume leadership is that not only can you affect the outcome of the group's deliberation, but you can also gain respect of the other participants for your contributions. Whether processor or leader, keep in mind you are a facilitator. You are helping the group to achieve its expressed objective. A facilitator, like the good salesperson, does not manipulate or play elaborate games to get his or her way. The facilitator involves others, encourages them to use their resources, and gets action from the group.

It might be helpful to jump ahead to describe some of the facilitating or informal leadership techniques you might employ.

Techniques for gaining control

There are techniques that enable you to gain or regain control, to get your ideas on the table once again. If you practice these techniques well, you will be seen by others as positive, supportive, helpful, and a leader. You also gain potential allies who will support you.

Mediating

Mediating is a useful technique when the spotlight is on people who are disputing one another's views. Mediating is not peacekeeping. A peacekeeper wants to minimize or wish away the conflict. There are people who say, "All right, keep calm" or "Let's not get carried away by feelings" or they will try to change the subject. All they usually accomplish is to erase the surface signs of turbulence. The strong emotions and the conflict continue unresolved.

Mediating acknowledges that the conflict exists. When you mediate, you step into the conflict and try to define the issues. Here is how you might make entry: "If I can interrupt, I'm getting the feeling that the issues are getting fuzzy, and I believe that it is important for me to understand how each of you sees them."

That's a good start. You don't directly charge them with straying from the issues, but you describe how hard it is for you to differentiate. Without laying fault at anyone's feet, you get the point across that the dispute is not as clear and helpful as it could and should be. Furthermore, by telling them that you want to understand the position that each one is taking, you compliment them. You bolster their self-esteem. This could be very important at this stage, because in a prolonged argument in front of others, the disputants often begin to believe that they are not being terribly effective and that their prestige might suffer as a result. So you reaffirm that their views are legitimate in your eyes, and you avoid any reinforcement of their suspicions that they have been making fools of themselves.

Your next step is to turn to disputant A and say, "What I hear you say is that you believe. . ." and then state what you have heard A say. It is very important to start your definition of the issues by announcing, "This is what I hear." That's a long way from saying, "This is what you said." Member A can argue about what he said, but you are the expert on what you have heard.

When you finish your summation, you ask A to verify the accuracy of your statements. Give A a chance to correct, subtract from, or add to. Then you turn to disputant B and repeat the technique. After B has had the same chance as A, you summarize the differences between them as you see them. Without being offensive, you have stopped the useless and even destructive wrangling, and you have gotten the group back on the issues. You've intervened, halting a bad situation, and created a possible good one in its stead. Don't be surprised to find that others in the group appreciate what you have done.

Incidentally, there is no reason you cannot take advantage of the situation to advance your own ideas. If you have already stated them, you now have a chance to restate them. For example, "That means that there are three approaches that have been suggested. Mine differs in that. . ." If you have not yet introduced your ideas, take time now. In other words, get the last or most recent word in. (When competitors have to make presentations, they vie for the last spot, because they know that the last presentation is usually remembered best.)

Harmonizing

Harmonizing is a less direct approach than mediating.

If your process-observing has led you to believe that the antagonists are not all that far apart or are actually near agreement, then you can emphasize the areas of near accord as you restate the positions of the adversaries. This is harmonizing. You are providing the group with some commonality that could form the base of a constructive discussion. Harmonizing is especially valuable when tempers are running high, or when the adversaries have become polarized.

You can take the technique one step further by underlining any of their views that are close to yours. Even if they differ from your position, you can now invite others to discuss the respective merits of theirs and yours. You have, in one stroke, broken a logjam and provided another opportunity for discussion of your ideas.

There are a number of other roles you can play that will build the group's respect for you and increase your influence in the group.

Supporting

Supporting is one of the most positive roles you can assume. You support another person's right to be heard, even though you may not necessarily agree with the content of that person's contribution. This is an approach to use with discretion. Generally, you would employ it if the group has not been receptive to new ideas, including your own. By working to get support for your colleague, you may succeed in opening the meeting up, and you may also enlist your colleague's support for getting your idea on the table. In supporting another, you may say, "I think that's a very interesting idea. We should talk about that." Or, "I'd like to know what others think." You can even make clear your non-agreement: "I'm not sure I agree, but it's something I hadn't thought of."

Competing

The opposite of supporting is competing. Interestingly, you can be both supportive and competitive in the same meeting. You support people's right to speak up, while you may not agree with their ideas. If the atmosphere is competitive, your support will be noticed and appreciated. Truly supportive people—that is, those who take a stand and make it possible for others to do so as well—are usually seen as personally secure people. People who perceive you as personally secure tend to be more receptive to your persuasive skills.

Listening

Listening is undoubtedly one of the most valuable skills you can bring to the conference table. People closely involved in a discussion sometimes have too much invested in their own feelings and opinions to hear clearly what others are saying. A question can be interpreted as an objection. A restatement of an idea in terms different from those originally used can be felt as opposition. For example, if someone counters Paul's point with a response that, you believe, misses Paul's point, you intervene: "That's not what I heard Paul saying." Then you give your interpretation, which will enjoy more credence than Paul's protests. You win two allies in one stroke by using your listening skills to make sure that valuable time is not spent debating points that were not made.

Expediting

When you expedite, you make sure that the gate is not closed to anyone. Some people have a hard time breaking into a vigorous discussion. For years I sat in on meetings with a woman who kept interjecting. "But . . . " "I don't think . . . " and such. People often ignored her and spoke right around her. Finally, at a break in the talking, she would say, "May I say something?"

Again, she would be ignored, until someone would say, "Martha has been trying to get a word in for the last ten minutes." That is expediting, and it is a technique that could be useful to you when others are monopolizing the discussion and you would like to open it up. If someone else is trying to enter the deliberation, your expediting that entry can serve to break up the monopoly (and open things up for you, too).

Summarizing

Summarizing is an extremely effective technique for taking control of a meeting. Meetings flounder when people don't listen well. They become inattentive, or their biases distort what they hear. Endless argument can occur, or people can talk all around a subject, with no one being persuaded of anything.

If you have been taking notes, you can intervene by saying, "Perhaps it might be useful to sum up what has been said so far." An expert summary, reasonably accurate and fair, opens the door for you: If the sides are polarized or inconclusive, then the atmosphere is ripe for you to step in with another option to consider. You've established that a gap exists. Now you fill it.

Undermining the group

The techniques described in the previous section are open and honest. You have a personal agenda, but you do not try to undermine the effectiveness of the group. On the other hand, manipulation and subterfuge do tend to undermine groups. If you were of a mind to manipulate the group, you would walk into the conference room with a predetermined objective and a firm resolve to achieve it at any cost. You might take the precaution of doing some selling ahead of time, lining up your allies. One of your first acts will be to determine who is with you and who is not. If you can create a powerful alliance, so much the better. You pretend to give consideration to differing viewpoints, but when you get the chance, you boost your side and try to keep the other side from presenting their arguments effectively.

I have seen people use humor to manipulate and undermine others. They make a joke: "Carl, I swear, when a new idea comes up, the first thing you think of is, 'How much will it cost?' One of these days Carl's going to come in here wearing a kilt." It's said with a smile, seemingly good naturedly. Others will laugh, perhaps even Carl. But his position, no matter how valid, has been weakened.

One manager I know always discounted the contributions of others by saying, "What's more important . . . " And you can always rely on the group manipulator to say, "Let's get back on the subject."

These are familiar shutting-off or putting-down devices. Their net result is often domination. They work. But in the long run, such techniques anger others, create distrust, and foster opposition. In the end, they are self-defeating.

You do not have to dominate, bully, or be underhanded to influence a group. You don't have to force. You can guide.

Getting the meeting going

The meeting has been going on for almost half an hour; nothing seems to be taking shape. People quibble over semantics, divert the discussion with anecdotes, ramble interminably. It is definitely time for someone to provide some leadership. And you have strong, clear ideas about how the group ought to move and in what direction. So now is the moment for you to take things in hand. Right?

Maybe yes, maybe no. If you are chairing the meeting, you don't want to look as if you are imposing your will, because that can lead to rebellion. If you are a member of the group, you don't want to appear to be challenging the status and position of the chairperson. Giving the impression that you are trying to take over may be resented by your peers, as well as by the group leader, who may find ways to repay you for that threat to his or her authority and image.

But you do want to have an impact. You have some ideas, and you'd like to get them on the table. When a conference seems to be drifting, there are acceptable ways to get it moving towards its goals. It all depends on your approach. For example:

Don't be impatient

You may assume nothing is happening because that's the way it looks on the surface. Yet people who are not accustomed to working together usually need a while to take each other's measure—garbage time, it's called—and a certain amount of noncommital, cautious, rambling talk helps them get to know one another and get a feeling for the various positions on issues that may develop. The content of such talk may not be significant, but if it results in group cohesiveness, the time is well spent. Consider this comparable to the pre-presentation warm-up time of the sales interview.

This initial period gives you a chance to test any currents that may be developing apart from the stated purpose of the meeting. For example, one person may be hoping to use the meeting to revive a proposal on a different subject that has been turned down previously. Such "hidden agendas" are often present in meetings.

Be low-key

You want the tacit consent of the group before you step in, and the way to get it is with a low-key approach. You can say something like: "I'd like to throw some ideas out and see what kinds of reactions you have." Getting the group's consent to your efforts to move it along does several things. You find out how ready the group is to go to work. It encourages everyone to listen carefully. And, you may get instant help from those who have been silently praying somebody would do something.

Keep your package simple

Introduce any ideas you have in brief, general form. Don't give people the impression that you have already worked everything out and that you were simply waiting for the right moment to take over. You can always flesh out the picture as others begin to respond to your suggestions.

Get others to help

Once you've gotten encouragement and support for your idea, get others to participate. Don't simply take over the meeting. To avoid the appearance of imposing your will on the group, let others discuss what you've offered. Support those who are interested in your ideas. Clarify your ideas when others seem unclear about them.

If your contributions don't take off, back away

Many people tend to press hard if they meet apathy or resistance. They argue and try to ramrod their idea through. But why bring the issue to the point of premature rejection? The group may not be ready to close yet. If you back off, you can regroup your forces and come in again when there seems to be a vacuum.

In fact, if you do meet resistance, you may be far from the close. You are probably still in the presentation phase, except that more than one presentation is being given. Use this time not only to get your ideas before the group but to do the following:

1. Know your prospects. Who's leaning which way? Who seems to be supporting or resisting you? Who could be your active ally?

2. Get people involved. You're going for a group close, and that's not likely to happen until the various members understand what you are selling. But you can't be sure they understand without getting them to participate. Be assertive *and* responsive.

3. Identify your competition. Who is in opposition to your ideas? Is he or she in stronger standing with the group? How hard will you have to work to best the competition?

In this stage of group deliberation, there is a lot more work to be done than just stating ideas. The leadership roles may be passed around. Use your chance wisely. Keep your statements short. People often tune out long, rambling speeches regardless of the worth of the content. Control your excitement, whether positive or negative. Take care not to shut other people off when they are speaking. Encourage others to talk. Listen attentively; make sure that others can see you are listening attentively, and that you respect the rights of others to present their views.

Traps to avoid

It is easy inadvertently to broadcast the message that you are *not* listening, that you do not respect the views of others. Furthermore, you may be totally unaware that others are reading that message in you.

Facial expression is a dead give-away. One executive I know makes it obvious when he disagrees with what is being said. He flashes a look which seems to say, "How can anyone believe such nonsense?" Worse yet, this executive doesn't seem to know that he displays such an expression. You must be alert to what your face is telling others. Otherwise you may unwittingly negate all of your previous efforts to influence your colleagues and to win their good will.

A show of impatience is another sign that you don't respect the views of others. Many meetings call for a great deal of tolerance and restraint. Another executive I know has a low tolerance for what she takes as rambling. She begins to shuffle papers, fidget, glance at her watch. The message thus communicated, is, "This fellow is not saying anything worth listening to, and I wish he'd finish in a hurry."

The result is that no one tries to pick up a salient thought from what is said. The minute the fidgeting starts, others around the table assume very blank faces. Undoubtedly some resent the presumed meaning of her nonverbal messages.

Another way people show impatience is to change the subject immediately after someone has spoken. The implication is "Forget what was just said. It doesn't count." It's an easy mistake to make—and a very costly one.

Talking through—interrupting and starting to speak before the other person has finished—is a common behavior. People get so carried away with a thought that it suddenly seems much more important than what is being said at the time. Sometimes it is. But the person interrupted will feel put down. The message conveyed is, "Don't bother with her. What she has to say isn't of any value. Listen to me."

Another type of interruption is when you make *sotto voce* comments to the person sitting in the next seat. Others in the group will turn their attention to what is going on in your corner rather than to the person who holds the floor.

The noisy sigh will surely cloud your prestige and influence with others. One manager I know will sigh deeply and look around the table. Once I asked her later what she was thinking of at the time, and she said she couldn't remember. But I recalled that the sigh came during a prolonged, rather boring impromptu speech given by a colleague. I don't know what she was thinking, but I do know how the sigh and the glare were interpreted: "This is all so boring."

I'm against doodling. It may broadcast no clear message—boredom, tension, impatience—but it does suggest that your mind is only partly on the proceedings.

Sit relaxed. You can take notes, which is complimentary to those who are talking (even if it is only a jotted word or two). Follow the discussion around the table. Nod, shake your head, smile as appropriate. These are normal behaviors and they indicate interest and involvement. Exhibit these behaviors as indiscriminately as possible. If you favor some members by nodding and smiling in their direction more frequently than in others', you may find yourself identified with a subgroup, and this identification may prejudice others against your ideas. Thus, regardless of how animated and intelligent any group of conferees may be in supporting you, try to maintain a separate identity. That is especially good advice if your supporting group is so obviously partisan that they ruffle other feathers around the table.

Losing your temper

One can be awfully provoked in a group, and it is sometimes easy to get angry at the sniping and carping that goes on. One executive told me of a report he had submitted. "It wasn't really very well done. I acknowledge that. But what annoyed me was the way people took it apart, literally sentence by sentence. I thought that was a bit much." So he withdrew the report, but in a rather dramatic way. He tore up the papers. "Years later," he says, "I'm still being reminded of that."

Sometimes when you feel that you are being attacked or you sense that the meeting has degenerated into sniping, your show of anger might accomplish a short-range purpose: stopping the ugliness. But it usually disrupts the meeting and puts everyone on edge. Your effectiveness is undermined. Long range, it can leave you with a reputation for hot-headedness. On the other hand, if there is general hostility and bad feelings lying just under the surface, your outburst may prove to be a detonation cap.

If the situation and the tension are intolerable, call for a recess. People *do* have to go to the rest room. If that isn't feasible, excuse yourself. Come back after you've calmed down.

Showing anger in a meeting is risky. It may relieve your tension while increasing that of the group. Also, when you lose control of yourself, you usually forfeit your chance to take control of the group.

Defeating the dominator

Someone may try to dominate the discussion at various stages of the meeting. When one person blatantly takes over meetings, there is usually a leadership vacuum. Whoever sits in the chair has, in effect, abdicated. What's more, the other members of the group are not working collectively to fill the gap. The one group member who moves in and take over then has an incentive to try the same tactics again, because they work.

In some cases, meetings which are unofficially run by a dominator achieve noteworthy results. And when that occurs, hard as it may be to accept, you have to consider this natural leader's contributions objectively. Unless you are certain of getting the same or better results, it might be wiser to suppress your irritation and accept the pattern that has emerged.

Frequently, though, the dominator subverts the meeting and turns it into an ego trip, ending in the group's acceptance of proposals that are not sufficiently thought through. When that happens, someone has to move, to exercise control. Here, first, are the ways *not* to proceed:

Don't take on the dominator one-to-one. A battle between the two of you, with everyone else as spectators, adds up to a performance, not a group discussion.

Don't leap into a negative role in countering the dominator's ideas. That can make you look obstructive.

Don't reinforce the dominator by withdrawing into silence. The takeover specialist will see that as acquiescence.

Instead, try employing these tactics:

Respond to others' ideas

If someone other than the dominator contributes a useful idea, start talking about it, even if you can't back it. Ask others for their opinions. This moves the spotlight from the dominator.

Direct your remarks to the group as a whole

At a meeting, people often talk only to the originator of an idea. But if you face others in the group as you talk and get them involved, even just as your audience, the chance for all-round participation is heightened.

Take every opportunity to ask questions

Direct your thoughts deliberately to the other participants, rather than to the dominator, and invite comments. The more you open the meeting up, the more you dilute the impact of the dominator. If the takeover specialist interrupts or tries to shut someone up, say, "Wait a minute. Gary didn't get to finish. I'd like to hear what he has to say." You are calling upon the resources of the group to deal with the one troublesome member.

If you must criticize, pick specific behaviors as your target

Before openly confronting the dominator, you had better be absolutely sure that you are acting for the group and have its support first. Furthermore, you are on more secure ground if you tie your criticism to specific behaviors: "Look, several times you've interrupted someone who was speaking. I wish you'd let people finish. It's frustrating for me not to get the complete thoughts." Or, "I get the feeling that you've already made up your mind that many of the ideas expressed here are not workable, but I'd like a chance to discuss them some more."

The problem is complicated by the fact that the dominator usually has much to offer the group—leadership, for instance. In some cases, too, the proposals that are rammed through are actually good ones, even though they would be improved by further discussion. So you don't want to destroy this person's usefulness; you want to channel that tremendous energy into helping the group get more of the results that *all* group members want.

The key to giving an off-the-cuff presentation

Eventually the group's deliberation will advance to the point at which another member looks at you and says, "I'd like to hear more about your idea." Other members reinforce the request. You're on. Perhaps you are prepared. Perhaps you are not. You are under pressure to present whether or not you have a presentation outlined.

How do you construct an instant presentation? One way is to remember this word: KEY. It will help you follow three steps in making an off-the-cuff presentation.

1. Make your key point (memory cue: K for key)

Give the bottom line, as they say, in the beginning. True, there is temptation to give an introduction or some background, but this creates impatience ("What's he getting at?"). Also, an introduction may ramble and this will spoil your impact, especially if people are getting weary of sitting and listening.

The best thing is to state clearly what you want: "As I mentioned before, I recommend that we try dispensing with the automatic investigation of applicants and investigate only those where the written data show certain gaps or discrepancies." Then follow up the key premise with something such as, "Now, let me tell you why I think we should test this."

2. Explain (memory cue: E for explanation)

Since this is impromptu, your explanation will give only the most important reasons. You may have developed seven, but three really have a wallop, so go for those three. There is no consensus among experts as to whether you should start with the most important or the least. Starting with the most important, you say, "There are a number of reasons why I've come to this conclusion, but by far the most impressive fact is . . ." Or if you go the other way, "Now, those first two points are in my view important, but what really pushed me over the line is . . ."

Don't spend too much time on each point. Too much explanation in an impromptu presentation may bore those who are interested. And the dangers of wandering off the track are great when you try to give a lengthy presentation without having thought it through.

3. *Wind up (memory cue: Y for wind up)*

Don't end abruptly, but don't sing *The Battle Hymn of the Republic*, either. A good bet is to insert a bit of a zinger in your windup. For example: "I realize there are some risks in this move, but I believe that if we test it on a representative group, we'll find out what we need to know. And if the test shows what I am convinced it will, we're all going to be heroes."

At the outset, take a moment to phrase your key point in your mind. A thoughtful, reflective pause can be very impressive, especially if you then state your key point slowly. When you explain, you may want to tick off your important points on your fingers. It makes the presentation livelier if you use natural gestures. And when you wind up, look at every person in the group, as if you were saying, "I want you to hear this, and I know that you are going to give it every consideration."

Keeping the decision decided

It is all too common for groups to end meetings with no decision, no action plan, except for some vague agreement to get together again. Be sure to close with a decision, even if it's only on a specific time for the next meeting. If possible, nail down the agenda for the next session. What preparatory work should the members do before the session? You might want to consult the previous chapter to review closing actions.

Once the decision ostensibly has been made, it still might not be in final form, or it might even be reversed. It is possible that people have second thoughts. Perhaps they weren't really sure when they made the decision. So, to minimize the damage of second thoughts, take the following steps:

Anticipate second thoughts

If reaching a decision involves much conflict, be ready for uncertainty after the decision has been made. if you suspect that some of the conflict has been concealed rather than resolved, and if you are in a position to delay the actual moment of decision, you may avoid future problems by trying to get at people's feelings about the alternatives now. You can help to create a more open climate by saying such things as, "I think we ought to take time to look at every option we can think of. Otherwise we could be cheating ourselves." This advice is easy to ignore when you are pressing hard for adoption of your own proposal. But if there is much unresolved conflict, you may have problems later getting people to carry out the decision that has been made in your favor.

Watch especially for signs that someone is pushing one course of action for reasons that appear emotional rather than rational. Also, some people press for early decisions because they find it difficult to sort through several alternatives. Putting undue pressure on the decision-maker or insisting on a quick decision when the issues are complex is more likely to lead to backtracking later.

Make it clear you are open to post-decision questions

During the decision-making phase, the idea often gets across that once the choice has been made, it will have to stick. There will be no turning back. Not surprisingly, this discourages bringing up later doubts in an open manner. But it doesn't discourage private questions about the wisdom of the choice or a reluctance to implement the decision with the degree of commitment needed to make it work.

Be prepared to listen

People who question a decision they have helped make may simply want an opportunity to voice their concern out loud. You may not have to "sell" them on the rightness of their original thinking because if you ask skillful and sympathetic questions that help them complete their thoughts, you can convey reassurance and encourage them to live happily with what they have decided.

Relying too heavily on rational arguments may lead you to overlook an emotional reaction that the decision has provoked. For example, what really worries the person you are talking to might be that the decision benefits someone he or she dislikes. Logic won't help in such cases, though giving time to discover the emotional factors involved and, if possible, the opportunity to talk them out may help.

Have facts at hand to reinforce the decision

Anecdotes involving the success of others who have gone this route (or who regrettably have not), statistics, a look ahead at the consequences of this approach versus that one can help doubters put their fears to rest.

The most effective role that any member of a group can play is that of facilitator, making it easier for the group to do what it has come together to do. As a facilitator, you have every right to advance your own ideas, proposals, and solutions. If you use good selling skills, you will not only have a better chance of getting them adopted by others but you will also have the satisfaction of knowing that you have accomplished this by being open, articulate, involving, and supportive. Your selling skills in group situations will, of course, help you to accomplish many of your immediate objectives, but perhaps even more important, they will establish you in the minds of others as credible, authoritative, reliable, and trustworthy—as a beneficial influence.

12

Selling and Successful Managing

While this book is intended for anyone who wishes to be more influential in any kind of organizational setting, it has a special message for managers of people. Today's work force is well-educated, independent, career-conscious, and mobile.

Employees don't automatically respond to a manager's I-want-this, you-do-that. They don't want to be told; they want to be sold. Why should I do it? they ask. What's in it for me? Many employees these days respond to motivating forces more than pressure from outside. They want more from their job than just a paycheck for services rendered—as no doubt you do, too.

The values of our contemporary work force distress some managers. They complain that managing people, getting a fair day's work, is much harder than it used to be. Employees seem to be less respectful of authority per se; they are as much concerned with their personal goals as with those of the organization, more insistent that their needs and wants be taken into consideration by management than in times past.

One-half of the complaint, in my judgment, is true. I believe that employees *are* more independent than their parents were as workers, and that they place a high value on their needs and wants. But the other half of the grousing—that managing is harder—I don't accept.

Most managers today have a better-educated, more skilled, more aware, and more involved force of employees than managers have ever before enjoyed. If those managers are not getting the results they want, then perhaps they had better look to their approach to managing.

To put it another way, envision employees as buyers and managers as sellers. American management has a superb, highly desirable product to sell. American employees, for the most part, are very willing, even anxious, customers. But the product has to be sold. And that is why I say that this book has a special message for people who manage people.

The product you sell your employees

What does the manager have in the way of a product to sell? Rewards for employee investment, to begin with. Most employees recognize that many of their personal goals and values can be realized through their work, whether those goals are to make money, get ahead professionally, achieve power and prestige, or something else. Work isn't something to be shunned or to be treated lightly; it isn't degrading or undesirable. Work for most people is the means by which they achieve what is important to them. For some people, the satisfaction of doing a good job is one of the most important rewards of all.

Motivation theory confirms this. All of the research regarding what motivates people at work points to this fact: people like to work. Work is very important in their lives. Most people want their work to be interesting, rewarding, and fulfilling. Most people want to have a sense of achievement. They want their work to have value, for themselves and for others.

Managers at nearly every level have the power, through the rewards that are at their disposal, to make work more rewarding and fulfilling for the people who report to them.

Managers want motivation and commitment from their employees. The manager wants the employee's motivating forces to be directed toward achieving the manager's goals. Managers can say to employees, "Look here, you give me what I need and want—my goals—and I'll give you what you want—rewards."

What are these rewards? Basically there are two types: internal and external.

External rewards

Mention external rewards and people immediately think of money. True, money is a reward, but most people do not regard money as the most important. In fact, some individuals don't even consider compensation a reward. Nor do some organizations; it is simply a cost of doing business.

There is a long list of things that people work for other than money. For example:

Growth

Surveys show that growth often heads the list of what employees want from their work. Most people want a sense of getting ahead, going from less interesting to more challenging tasks and responsibilities. It is a rare employee who does not get satisfaction out of knowing more and being more skilled this year than last. Social psychologists studying people at work demonstrate clearly in their research that not only do most employees not shun responsibility, they seek it.

There are countless opportunities for managers to say to hardworking employees, "You've done so well in your assigned tasks, it's time for you to take on a more difficult or more challenging job. You deserve it." Or, "Perhaps you'd like to expand your skills through more training. We'll pick up the tab." Often it isn't even a matter of spending money to provide growth opportunities. All you have to do is reassign the work.

Freedom

As people grow more skilled and confident, they usually wish to have more freedom over how they do their work—methods, scheduling, priorities, hours worked, etc. In any list of perceived rewards that employees supply, freedom over the work ranks high. When the manager eases up on controls, thereby transferring control to employees, the message is: "I recognize that you have been doing a good job, and I am confident that you'll continue that good job."

Praise

Praise doesn't cost money, and the manager has an inexhaustible supply of it. People like to have their good work recognized. If you are a manager and do not consistently recognize the work that meets your standards with some form of private or public praise, you are missing a very big payoff. Consistent, specific, proportionate praise accomplishes magnificent things.

Perks

Of course, there is money. Promotion is important, too (although not to everyone). There are many other ways to recognize good performance—a business trip, time off, new furniture in the office, a desirable transfer, a better office or work location, first crack at the most desirable tasks, etc.

If you can't list, in about ten minutes, fifteen or twenty ways to let employees know that they are doing a good job, then you might not know your product. And the first maxim of selling is *know your product*—the rewards you can give.

Internal rewards

Some rewards are generated by the employees, not by the manager. For example, the satisfaction of doing good work, a sense of achievement of a difficult goal, or the increased self-esteem that comes from acquiring a new skill are all rewards that come from within. But you, the manager, can enhance these internal rewards. Take the case of an employee who has a "win" orientation, who likes competition. You would want to assign such a person to especially challenging work with high visibility and high goals so that he would have a chance to excel. Another employee has what are called high social needs. You would want to make sure that she had tasks to do that brought her into extensive contact with others, to work with them and be accepted by them. Still another employee is turned on by feeling more professionally competent, so you would give her opportunities in her work to expand that competence. Some employees strive for status—for example, to be the most experienced or versatile in a work group. You would make sure that these people have sufficient chances to demonstrate these abilities. Different strokes for different folks, as they used to say. However, knowing what tasks to assign to which employees leads to the next maxim: *know your prospect.*

Knowing the prospect

For the manager, knowing the prospect is just as important as knowing the product. You may be well acquainted with all the kinds of rewards at your disposal, but if you do not know how to use them—if you don't know which prospects are likely to be attracted by which rewards—your effectiveness is severely limited.

You may not know specifically all of the personal goals, values, and interests of each of your employees. But through watching them, setting standards and goals with them, measuring the results of their efforts, and listening to their requests, you should have a general idea of what appeals to them on the job. Which employees are highly competitive, ambitious, interested in security more than mobility, anxious to earn the esteem of others, seeking identity with the group (high affiliation needs), have an entrepreneurial spirit? Shape their tasks and assignments to their needs.

Your employees are your prospects. If you have little or no idea of their wants and needs, then you will have a hard time matching your rewards to their goals, your product to their needs. The worst that can happen is to have your sales story fall on deaf ears. You are wasting your time and energy if you do not know their buying motivations.

Involving your prospects

There are several ways in which you involve your employees. If you
have a goal-setting program, such as Management by Objectives
(MBO), you should enlist their participation in setting those goals.
But you do not need organization-wide MBO to get employees involved in your goals. Departmental goals should not be imposed
upon employees. They should have a say in defining them. Sometimes employees know better than you what goals are realistic for
them, and often they will suggest objectives that are higher than the
ones you would set on your own.

The goals you and your employees set should form the base for
your performance appraisal system. Each appraisal period, from six
to twelve months, sit down with the employee to evaluate how he
or she has done during the last period in light of the goals the two
of you established. Then set goals for the forthcoming period of
evaluation.

From these periodic evaluations, you can certainly glean what
kinds of work the employee can do best. Furthermore, you should
encourage the employee to set goals for personal development—
what education or training is desired, what skills can be strengthened, what new skills can be acquired. Personal goals can give you
another needed insight into the interests, values, and directions of
the employee.

Coaching is another tool that the manager can use to learn more
about the prospect. Coaching has at least two functions. One is to
help the employee work through a problem related to the job. For
example, if an unexpected development creates a crisis, the manager
coaches the employee through it to a solution. But there is another,
longer range reason for coaching: the growth and development of
the employee. Periodically, manager and employee should sit down
together to discuss ways in which the employee can advance, can
become more effective and capable. Here especially the manager
has an excellent opportunity to determine what aspects of his product
the employee is most interested in buying. In coaching for growth,
the manager helps the employee chart the future and the means to

get there. It is a positive, forward-thinking step that helps the manager in setting goals and assigning tasks with the employee.

Don't overlook the value of criticism as a technique for involving employees. When employees are not doing the level of work that has been agreed upon, they are probably as unhappy as you are. Sitting down with them and showing them what is deficient and how to correct it can get them on the track to their goals again. At the same time, you are recognizing their need to know how they are doing.

Getting the performance you want

Are you prepared for opposition from your prospects, the employees who report to you? Sometimes it is intentional. People may balk at certain tasks and assignments. They may reduce their efforts on the job because they feel discriminated against. They may lose motivation for personal reasons: illness, family distractions, money concerns, and so on.

But very often, the opposition is inadvertent. Employees who do not perform well may be victims of misunderstanding. They don't know what is expected of them, or they don't know how to do the work. There may be any number of reasons they do not work well even though they wish to do so.

This is a prime time for selling skills on your part. You, as manager, need to be patient as you seek information. What is the real reason for the dip in performance? Counseling an employee with a performance problem demands the same kind of skill that is required of the salesperson trying to find out what is preventing the prospect from buying. You must first work toward getting an agreement from the employee that a problem exists: the work is not being done as it should be. Once the employee and you are in agreement on that, you can look for a solution together. The employee, remember, brings certain strengths and needs to the counseling session. Recognizing them and involving the employee will help you to overcome any "opposition."

Here are three points that constitute my most frequently voiced counsel to managers:

1. Tell employees what you expect of them. Unfortunately managers too often assume that employees know what the manager wants in the way of goals, standards, deadlines, and so on. It just isn't true. Managers must be very explicit.

2. Give on-going feedback on how well your employees are doing. When employees are trying to do what you expect, they need to know if they are on the right track or not. A frequent complaint is that employees hear only when they foul up, not when they do a good job. I once knew a manager whose type, I'm afraid, is legion. His employees never knew quite what he wanted, but they received a lot of feedback when they didn't give it to him. His lack of positive guidance was very frustrating for them.

3. When they have done what you want, reward them. And make sure the rewards are consistently given.

If you make a point of observing all three points, you will readily get the action that you expect to get. Every time you assign a task, give a new job, or set goals, you get an agreement on what is to be done. You have made a contract with your employees. Because employees know that you will honor the contract, they will live up to their end. They may not always know in advance how you will reward them, but they are confident that you will do so in some appropriate way. Their trust in you and your credibility with them are the cornerstones of your persuasiveness.

The manager of motivation

As we've seen, motivation theory applies across the board. Whether the decision is to buy a specific product or service, or to commit oneself to a particular job or assignment, the considerations are much the same. People will choose those ends (rewards) that are the most valuable to them. Thus, confronted with three alternatives, we will select the one of greatest personal value, *all other things being equal*. This is a crucial qualifier, because personal value is not our only motivating factor. Ability to do what the choice requires is equally important. As an employee, I probably will not take on a task that I perceive as too difficult for me. As a buyer, I will not sign my name on the dotted line if the purchase is going to raise a lot of difficulties. Ease, feasibility, availability, and probability are all important words in motivating others, as they are in selling.

As a manager, you can create an environment that motivates your staff and is conducive to high performance. In assigning tasks, setting goals, giving feedback, you find ways to recognize your employee's needs and personal objectives. You show that you are concerned, that their needs are met and their rewards achieved, as yours are. You act as a resource. You provide constructive working conditions, coaching and training, counseling, encouragement, and whatever other factors will enhance the value of the job in the eyes of employees or add to their confidence that they can do it well.

Your selling skills are just as important in your dealings with peers and higher executives. Today's managers, whatever their level, are being given more and more responsibility and discretion. As a result, it takes more and more negotiating to achieve goals and gain cooperation. One manager cannot demand that another cooperate with him. It is much more a matter of one manager persuading another that it is in the interest of both to work together.

As authority and decision-making in organizations become decentralized, as the baby boom enters management ranks, and as more people work longer before retiring, competition for the top positions becomes keener. Jungle fighters do not often make it to the top. What is required, among other things, is skill in interpersonal transactions.

Finally, as the emphasis on self-fulfillment in careers increases, people need not only to define their goals but to work out methods of achieving those goals. And that usually involves other people.

Few objectives on the work scene can be accomplished without the active participation of others.

The person who goes far today is the one who knows how to work effectively with other people, who is skillful in winning what he or she needs from those with whom they work. And the foundation of skills in dealing with others can be found in basic selling techniques. There is just as much selling required inside an organization as outside.

Index